T0172953

Louis J. Kruger
Editor

Computers in the Delivery of Special Education and Related Services: Developing Collaborative and Individualized Learning Environments

Computers in the Delivery of Special Education and Related Services: Developing Collaborative and Individualized Learning Environments has been co-published simultaneously as *Special Services in the Schools*, Volume 17, Numbers 1/2 2001.

More advance
REVIEWS, COMMENTARIES, EVALUATIONS . . .

"**T**his book addresses the cutting-edge application of computers in special services in the schools. The articles discuss research regarding the effectiveness of computer use in a number of applications, including curriculum-based measurement, consultation, instruction, Internet and e-mail interprofessional collaboration, and school-based consultation teams. The papers reflect the analysis of the effectiveness of the use of computer-assisted instruction and communication, and conclude that when appropriately utilized they make a qualitative difference. The authors challenge special service professionals to use computers reflectively, in a constructivist manner, and continually assess and evaluate the effectiveness of a tool. Rather than blindly advocating the application of computer use in all situations, these research articles demonstrate the need for data-based decision making in the adoption of computer-assisted techniques."

Virginia Smith Harvey, PhD
Dean
Graduate College of Education
University of Massachusetts, Boston

"**C**omputers in the Delivery of Special Education and Related Services* is a scholarly and authoritative compilation. It will help school psychologists and special education staff to bridge the gap between scientific theory and daily practice. Each chapter describes the promise and the pitfalls of technology from the viewpoint of people who are on the 'front lines' every day. Yet the emphasis is on people, relationships, and improving the lives of children–not on technical descriptions of hardware. This book will rejuvenate your creativity and spark several new ideas for improving your work in schools!"

Philip B. Bowser, NCSP
School Psychologist
Roseburg Public Schools
Oregon

"**D**r. Kruger's book is a wonderful resource for all educators. It provides a blueprint for incorporating computer technology into the special education setting, and how its use can be individualized for different students. Dr. Kruger demonstrates how computer technology can benefit students, teachers, and families. Examples of how to incorporate computer technology into an educational program are provided. Using Dr. Kruger's guidelines, one can immediately begin to develop strategies for making use of computer technology in their particular setting.

Several chapters were of particular interest. In 'Using E-Mail to Collaborate with Professionals and Parents,' the authors demonstrate how through e-mail, obstacles to communication can be overcome, and collaboration can be faciliated. 'Family and Related Service Partnerships' is particularly valuable; it cautions that families of varying socio-economic and ethnic backgrounds may perceive computer technology differently, and provides thoughtful recommendations for professionals to consider as they integrate computer technology into the educational program of students."

Barry S. Barbarasch, EdD
School Psychologist
Hamilton Township Schools
New Jersey

The Haworth Press, Inc.

Computers in the Delivery of Special Education and Related Services: Developing Collaborative and Individualized Learning Environments

Computers in the Delivery of Special Education and Related Services: Developing Collaborative and Individualized Learning Environments has been co-published simultaneously as *Special Services in the Schools*, Volume 17, Numbers 1/2 2001.

The *Special Services in the Schools* Monographic "Separates"

Below is a list of "separates," which in serials librarianship means a special issue simultaneously published as a special journal issue or double-issue *and* as a "separate" hardbound monograph. (This is a format which we also call a "DocuSerial.")

"Separates" are published because specialized libraries or professionals may wish to purchase a specific thematic issue by itself in a format which can be separately cataloged and shelved, as opposed to purchasing the journal on an on-going basis. Faculty members may also more easily consider a "separate" for classroom adoption.

"Separates" are carefully classified separately with the major book jobbers so that the journal tie-in can be noted on new book order slips to avoid duplicate purchasing.

You may wish to visit Haworth's website at . . .

http://www.HaworthPress.com

. . . to search our online catalog for complete tables of contents of these separates and related publications.

You may also call 1-800-HAWORTH (outside US/Canada: 607-722-5857), or Fax 1-800-895-0582 (outside US/Canada: 607-771-0012), or e-mail at:

getinfo@haworthpressinc.com

Computers in the Delivery of Special Education and Related Services: Developing Collaborative and Individualized Learning Environments, edited by Louis J. Kruger, PsyD (Vol. 17, No. 1/2, 2001). *"An excellent compendium. . . . The topics selected cover a broad conceptual spectrum, yet provide specific and useful information for the practitioner. A valuable resource for professionals at all levels. I highly recommend it." (David G. Gotthelf, PhD, Director of Student Services, Lincoln-Sudbury Regional School District, Massachusetts)*

Inclusion Practices with Special Needs Students: Theory, Research, and Application, edited by Steven I. Pfeiffer, PhD, ABPP, and Linda A. Reddy, PhD (Vol. 15, No. 1/2, 1999). *Provides a much needed and balanced perspective of the issues faced by educators committed to understanding how to best serve children with disabilities in schools.*

Emerging School-Based Approaches for Children with Emotional and Behavioral Problems: Research and Practice in Service Integration, edited by Robert J. Illback, PsyD, and C. Michael Nelson, EdD (Vol. 10, No. 2, and Vol. 11, No. 1/2, 1996). *"A stimulating and valuable contribution to the topic." (Donald K. Routh, PhD, Professor of Psychology, University of Miami)*

Educational Outcomes for Students with Disabilities, edited by James E. Ysseldyke, PhD, and Martha L. Thurlow (Vol. 9, No. 2, 1995). *"Clearly directed at teaching staff, psychologists, and other educationists but has relevance to all who work with children and young people with disabilities in schools of further education. . . . A useful book." (Physiotherapy)*

Promoting Student Success Through Group Interventions, edited by Joseph E. Zins, EdD, and Maurice J. Elias, PhD (Vol. 8, No. 1, 1994). *"Contains clear, concise, and practical descriptions of a variety of group interventions designed to promote students' success in school and life." (Social Work with Groups Newsletter)*

Promoting Success with At-Risk Students: Emerging Perspectives and Practical Approaches, edited by Louis J. Kruger, PsyD (Vol. 5, No. 3/4, 1990). *"Essential to professionals interested in new developments in the education of at-risk students, guidelines for implementation of approaches, and the prevention of student crises and discipline problems." (Virginia Child Protection Newsletter)*

Leadership and Supervision in Special Services: Promising Ideas and Practices, edited by Leonard C. Burrello, EdD, and David E. Greenburg, EdD (Vol. 4, No. 1/2, 1988). *A rich source of ideas for administrative personnel involved in the delivery of special educational programs and services to children with handicapping conditions.*

School-Based Affective and Social Interventions, edited by Susan G. Forman, PhD (Vol. 3, No. 3/4, 1988). *"Provides a valuable starting point for the psychologist, counselor, or other special service provider, special educator, regular classroom teacher, nurse, vice-principal, or other administrator who is willing to get involved in the struggle to help children and adolescents feel good about themselves and get along better in this world." (Journal of Pediatric Nursing)*

Facilitating Cognitive Development: International Perspectives, Programs, and Practices, edited by Milton S. Schwebel and Charles A. Maher, PsyD (Vol. 3, No. 1/2, 1986). *Experts discuss the vital aspects of programs and services that will facilitate cognitive development in children and adolescents.*

Emerging Perspectives on Assessment of Exceptional Children, edited by Randy Elliot Bennett, EdD, and Charles A. Maher, PsyD (Vol. 2, No. 2/3, 1986). *"Contains a number of innovative and promising approaches to the topic of assessment. It is an important addition to the rapidly changing field of special education and should be read by any individual who is interested in the assessment of exceptional children."* *(Journal of Psychological Assessment)*

Health Promotion in the Schools: Innovative Approaches to Facilitating Physical and Emotional Well-Being, edited by Joseph E. Zins, Donald I. Wagner, and Charles A. Maher, PsyD (Vol. 1, No. 3, 1985). *"Examines new approaches to promoting physical and emotional well-being in the schools. . . . A good introduction to new-style health education."* *(Curriculum Review)*

Microcomputers and Exceptional Children, edited by Randy Elliot Bennett, EdD, and Charles A. Maher, PsyD (Vol. 1, No. 1, 1984). *"This volume provides both the experienced and novice micro buff with a solid overview of the potential and real uses of the technology with exceptional students."* *(Alex Thomas, PhD, Port Clinton, Ohio)*

ALL HAWORTH BOOKS AND JOURNALS
ARE PRINTED ON CERTIFIED
ACID-FREE PAPER

Computers in the Delivery of Special Education and Related Services: Developing Collaborative and Individualized Learning Environments

Louis J. Kruger

Editor

Computers in the Delivery of Special Education and Related Services: Developing Collaborative and Individualized Learning Environments has been co-published simultaneously as *Special Services in the Schools*, Volume 17, Numbers 1/2 2001.

The Haworth Press, Inc.
New York • London • Oxford

Computers in the Delivery of Special Education and Related Services: Developing Collaborative and Individualized Learning Environments has been co-published simultaneously as *Special Services in the Schools*, Volume 17, Numbers 1/2 2001.

The development, preparation, and publication of this work has been undertaken with great care. However, the publisher, employees, editors, and agents of The Haworth Press and all imprints of The Haworth Press, Inc., including The Haworth Medical Press® and Pharmaceutical Products Press®, are not responsible for any errors contained herein or for consequences that may ensue from use of materials or information contained in this work. Opinions expressed by the author(s) are not necessarily those of The Haworth Press, Inc.

The Haworth Press, Inc., 10 Alice Street, Binghamton, NY 13904-1580 USA

Cover design by Thomas J. Mayshock Jr.

Library of Congress Cataloging-in-Publication Data

Computers in the delivery of special education and related services: developing collaborative and individualized learning environments / Louis J. Kruger, editor.
      p. cm.
      "Has been co-published simultaneously as Special services in the schools, volume 17, numbers 1/2 2001."
      Includes bibliographical references and index.
      ISBN 0-7890-1182-4 (alk. paper) – ISBN 0-7890-1183-2 (alk. paper)
      1. Handicapped children–Education–United States. 2. Computer-assisted instruction–United States. I. Kruger, Louis J. II. Special services in the schools.

LC4024 .C645 2001
371.9'04334–dc21
                                                                 00-047245

Indexing, Abstracting & Website/Internet Coverage

   This section provides you with a list of major indexing & abstracting services. That is to say, each service began covering this periodical during the year noted in the right column. Most Websites which are listed below have indicated that they will either post, disseminate, compile, archive, cite or alert their own Website users with research-based content from this work. (This list is as current as the copyright date of this publication.)

(continued)

Special Bibliographic Notes related to special journal issues (separates) and indexing/abstracting:

- indexing/abstracting services in this list will also cover material in any "separate" that is co-published simultaneously with Haworth's special thematic journal issue or DocuSerial. Indexing/abstracting usually covers material at the article/chapter level.
- monographic co-editions are intended for either non-subscribers or libraries which intend to purchase a second copy for their circulating collections.
- monographic co-editions are reported to all jobbers/wholesalers/approval plans. The source journal is listed as the "series" to assist the prevention of duplicate purchasing in the same manner utilized for books-in-series.
- to facilitate user/access services all indexing/abstracting services are encouraged to utilize the co-indexing entry note indicated at the bottom of the first page of each article/chapter/contribution.
- this is intended to assist a library user of any reference tool (whether print, electronic, online, or CD-ROM) to locate the monographic version if the library has purchased this version but not a subscription to the source journal.
- individual articles/chapters in any Haworth publication are also available through the Haworth Document Delivery Service (HDDS).

Computers in the Delivery of Special Education and Related Services: Developing Collaborative and Individualized Learning Environments

CONTENTS

ABOUT THE EDITOR

Louis J. Kruger, PsyD, is Associate Professor at Northeastern University, where he is director of the specialist level program in school psychology, and a faculty member of the combined doctoral level program in school and counseling psychology. His areas of interest are teamwork, Internet communities, computer-mediated collaboration, and organizational change. Dr. Kruger is Founder of the Global School Psychology Network (www.dac.neu.edu/cp/consult), a professional development community on the Internet, and Co-Director of the Global Early Intervention Network, another Internet community (www.dac.neu.edu/cp/ei).

An Overview

During the last two decades, we have witnessed staggering advancements in computer technology. This is particularly evident in regard to the Internet. Twenty years ago, e-mail was used by a small group of scientists and academics. Now, the Internet and computer-mediated communication (i.e., digital text, audio, or video transmitted over a network) are inching toward encompassing all previous means of communication. In 1984, Bennett and Maher presciently commented that computers were on the verge of transforming special services in the schools. The transformation is now in full bloom, as the chapters in this edited volume reflect assessment, instruction, and communication.

Despite the transformative potential of computers, there are concerns about their possible negative effects. In this regard, a chief concern is that using a computer is a solitary activity, and therefore might lead to greater isolation of individuals. This concern is particularly salient for students with special needs, many of whom have deficits in social skills, and may be isolated from peers. In addition, Vygotsky (1978) and others maintain that learning and development of competence is more likely to occur in an interpersonal context, such as with an esteemed mentor or teacher. Another concern is that computers lack the flexibility to treat people as individuals, and as a result there will be a lack of attention to students' specific needs. Given that the education of students with special needs is predicated on developing individualized educational programs, this is a particularly important concern to special services providers. A third concern is that computers might facilitate rote learning, but won't help foster good

[Haworth indexing entry note]: "An Overview." Kruger, Louis J. Published in *Computers in the Delivery of Special Education and Related Services: Developing Collaborative and Individualized Learning Environments* (ed: Louis J. Kruger) The Haworth Press, Inc., 2001, pp. xiii-xv. Single or multiple copies of this article are available for a fee from The Haworth Document Delivery Service [1-800-342-9678, 9:00 a.m. - 5:00 p.m. (EST). E-mail address: getinfo@haworthpressinc.com].

xiii

problem-solving skills; and these skills are essential to promoting independence and life-long learning. The authors of the chapters in this edited book review research and provide examples that address these concerns, as well as illustrate how computers can enhance individualization, collaboration, and problem-solving skills. Thus, the most significant change that has occurred in the last 15 years might be in the way people perceive the potential of computers. Previously presumed limitations of the technology might turn out to be its areas of strength!

In the first chapter, Fuchs and Fuchs review research on how computer software has been used to facilitate the assessment of students' progress within specific curricula. In particular, they marshal convincing evidence which suggests that computer software can overcome obstacles to teachers using curriculum-based measurement, such as the time involved in collecting, summarizing, and drawing instructional implications from the data. Fuchs and Fuchs argue that individualized instruction also can be time efficient.

In the next chapter, Woodward discusses the importance of embedding technology in a sound pedagogical context. By means of case examples, he demonstrates how widely available technologies, such as calculators and computer spreadsheets, can be used to develop problem-solving skills among academically at-risk students. Woodward conveys the excitement of these students as they use mathematical skills to solve "real-world" problems.

The third chapter, by O'Neill, focuses on how the Internet can be used to access resources beyond the walls of the classroom. In particular, he discusses how students can use the Internet to discuss class projects with experts, who can help students "ask the right questions" rather than merely provide answers. Within the context of these "telementoring" relationships between experts and students, O'Neill provides examples of how problem-solving assistance can be to tailored to the individual students' needs.

In the next chapter, Ryba, Selby, and Kruger discuss how the Internet can be used to create new types of learning communities for both students as well as professionals. They extend Vygotsky's notion of "zone of proximal development" (ZPD) to the community level; postulating a "collective" ZPD, whereby the experienced users mentor the on-line novices. Ryba, Selby and Kruger also provide guidelines for developing Internet-based learning communities.

In the following chapter, Macklem, Kruger, and Struzziero discuss how e-mail might might be used to complement and strengthen face-to-face collaboration, including consultations between teachers and special services providers. Based on a review of the research, they discuss possible advantages and disadvantages of the medium. Macklem, Kruger, and Struzziero provide examples of how e-mail might be incorporated into consultation.

Next, Parette and Anderson provide an insightful analysis of the factors involved with home computer use to address a student's special needs. They illuminate the importance of understanding the family's values, expectations, and cultural background before proceeding to make recommendations about home computer use. Parette and Anderson present a useful list of questions that service providers should keep in mind when collaborating with parents in regard to home computer use.

In the final chapter, Aldrich discusses school-based consultation teams, and software that might facilitate the work of these teams. He points out common problems with school-based teams. Building upon a systematic approach to consultation, Aldrich shows how software can help a team through specific aspects of the problem-solving process, including collecting data, selecting interventions, documenting team decisions, and providing follow-up.

Collectively, these chapters reflect the hope that the creative use of computers will transcend whatever nagging stereotypes that have been assigned to them, and be viewed as partners in the educational process; machines that enhance current practices, and open new vistas for learning and collaboration.

Louis J. Kruger

REFERENCES

Bennett, R.E., & Maher, C.A. (Eds.). (1984). Microcumputers and exceptional children. (Special Issue) *Special Services in the Schools 1,* (1).

Vygotsky, L.S. (1978). *Mind and society.* Cambridge, UK: Cambridge University Press.

Computer Applications
to Curriculum-Based Measurement

Lynn S. Fuchs
Douglas Fuchs

Peabody College of Vanderbilt University

SUMMARY. Students learn more when teachers individually tailor student programs using curriculum-based measurement (CBM) to inform instructional planning. Given the demonstrated efficacy of CBM, along with teachers' difficulty in implementing this method, we have developed and researched computer applications to CBM. In this article, we describe these computer applications and provide examples of how the technology has been used; then, we provide an overview of the research we have conducted to examine its utility. We discuss implications for the field of special education. *[Article copies available for a fee from The Haworth Document Delivery Service: 1-800-342-9678. E-mail address: <getinfo@haworthpressinc.com> Website: <http://www.HaworthPress.com>]*

KEYWORDS. Assessment, curriculum-based measurement, computers

In developing curriculum-based measurement (CBM), Deno (1985) sought to design a measurement system that teachers could use efficiently to produce accurate, meaningful information for indexing stu-

---

Address correspondence to: Lynn S. Fuchs, Box 328 Peabody, Vanderbilt University, Nashville, TN 37203.

Research described in this article was supported in part by Grant Nos. H180E20004, H023E90020, H023A10010, G008730087, and G008530198 from the U.S. Department of Education, Office of Special Education, to Vanderbilt University. Statements should not, however, be interpreted as official policy of the agencies.

[Haworth co-indexing entry note]: "Computer Applications to Curriculum-Based Management." Fuchs, Lynn S., and Douglas Fuchs. Co-published simultaneously in *Special Services in the Schools* (The Haworth Press, Inc.) Vol. 17, No. 1/2, 2001, pp. 1-14; and: *Computers in the Delivery of Special Education and Related Services: Developing Collaborative and Individualized Learning Environments* (ed: Louis J. Kruger) The Haworth Press, Inc., 2001, pp. 1-14. Single or multiple copies of this article are available for a fee from The Haworth Document Delivery Service [1-800-342-9678, 9:00 a.m. - 5:00 p.m. (EST). E-mail address: getinfo@haworthpressinc.com].

1

dents' development of academic competence. The goal was to provide teachers with technically sound classroom-based assessment that could answer questions about the effectiveness of programs and help teachers plan better instructional programs.

Research on CBM (for a review, see Fuchs & Fuchs, 1998) indicates that CBM can help teachers individualize instruction, plan better programs, and effect superior academic growth among students with and without disabilities (Fuchs, Deno, & Mirkin, 1984; Fuchs, Fuchs, Hamlett, & Ferguson, 1992; Fuchs, Fuchs, Hamlett, & Stecker, 1991; Jones & Krouse, 1988; Wesson, 1991). With CBM, the special educator plans an initial instructional program, and while implementing that program, conducts CBM routinely to monitor the extent to which the student is learning. The teacher uses the ongoing assessment to tailor an instructional program over time that does, in fact, produce superior learning for the student.

For example, consider Figure 1, which shows Melissa Jones's CBM performance over time on fifth-grade reading passages. Twice each week, Melissa takes a CBM maze test, which presents her with a fifth-grade passage, from which every seventh word has been deleted; for each blank, Melissa sees three words that might fit in the passage (only one of which is a sensible replacement). Melissa has 3 minutes to quietly read aloud, while selecting words to replace the blanks. On each CBM, her score is the number of correct replacements, which is represented on her graph with a dot (see Figure 1). At the beginning of the year (see first three dots), Melissa scored approximately 12 correct replacements. Based on this score and normative CBM information indicating that students typically grow by approximately .5 correct replacements per week, the teacher established Melissa's end-of-year goal as 27 correct replacements (signified on the graph with a "G"). A goal line, connecting Melissa's baseline performance of 12 to her end-of-year goal of 27, is represented on the graph as a dotted diagonal line. The teacher uses this goal line to evaluate, on any given day, the adequacy of Melissa's progress toward achieving the goal. In Individual Education Program (IEP) terms, the first three dots are Melissa's "current performance level"; the end-of-year goal, her "long-term goal"; and the goal line, her "short-term objective." Because the student's IEP is graphically displayed on a CBM graph, the IEP becomes a "living document" that teachers can use to inform instructional decision making in the following ways.

FIGURE 1. Example of an Individual Student's Computer-Generated CBM Graph in Reading

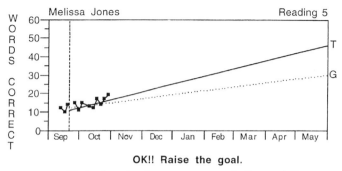

OK!! Raise the goal.
Student's rate of progress exceeds the goal line

First, as shown on Melissa's graph, when the student's actual rate of progress (represented by the solid diagonal trend line) predicts that the student will exceed the goal (see "T" on the graph), the CBM recommendation is for the teacher to raise the goal (see bottom of Figure 1). Second, in a similar way, whenever the student's trend line predicts that the student will fail to achieve the goal, the CBM recommendation is for the teacher to revise the instructional program to stimulate greater progress. Third, for mathematics computation, for mathematics concepts and applications, and for spelling, teachers can conduct a CBM skills analysis. CBM Skills analyses identify the skills, within the CBM annual curriculum, on which students qualify as mastered (black boxes), almost mastered (black boxes with a dot), partially mastered (checkered boxes), not mastered (striped boxes), and not tried (white boxes). (See Figure 2, page 2, for a skills analysis within the CBM classwide report.) Teachers can use CBM skills analyses to identify the content on which students require additional instruction.

Unfortunately, despite CBM's demonstrated efficacy for these kinds of instructional decision making, teachers frequently do not use CBM. At least two reasons explain teachers' reluctance (Fuchs, Fuchs, Hasselbring, & Hamlett, 1987; Wesson, King, & Deno, 1984). First, substantial time is necessary to collect and manage CBM. Teachers must prepare test materials, administer and score tests, and graph and analyze scores. Second, teachers often find it difficult to translate assessments into instructional improvements that can be implemented feasibly.

Consequently, we have conducted a research program to explore how computers can be used to surmount these difficulties. In this article, we describe CBM software, illustrate its use, and provide an overview of the research we have conducted exploring its utility. Then, we discuss implications for the fields of special education.

DESCRIPTION OF CBM AND CBM SOFTWARE

We have developed CBM software in reading, spelling, and mathematics (i.e., computation, concepts and applications, and problem solving). In each area, this software has three inter-related functions: (1) automatic data collection, scoring, and student feedback, (2) automatic data management, and (3) automatic feedback and instructional recommendations to teachers.

Students use CBM software during automatic data collection, scoring, and student feedback. The computer administers the CBM while the student works at the computer; the student enters responses into the software as the assessment is completed. For example, in reading, the computer presents the CBM to the student with a maze. The student works at the computer, reading quietly aloud while using the mouse to restore correct words to the passage. After two and one-half minutes, the computer removes the passage and shows the student that day's score (number of correct replacements) and a graph of the scores over time. The student's work and score are saved and organized for teacher feedback.

The teacher simply reviews the data stored by the computer. Analyses provide detailed individual performance descriptions and class-wide information. Figure 1 shows an example of a computer-generated *individual student's analysis* in reading. As explained in the case study, the dark diagonal line is the student's trend line, which predicts that the student will exceed her IEP goal. The computer, therefore, recommends that the teacher raise the goal. Figure 2 illustrates a 5-page CBM *class report* (these are sample pages; for a complete report, contact the authors). Page 1 of the class report presents graphs showing scores over time for the 25th, 50th, and 75th percentile of the class; students whose performance currently falls below the 25th percentile of the class; areas in which the whole class has improved during the past month; areas in which the class might profit from large-group instruction; and areas in which students might profit from small-group instruction. Page 2 provides supplementary information, with a skills profile in computation. Page 3 presents a class roster of recent CBM scores and slopes (weekly rates of improvement over time). Page 4 offers suggestions about how to pair students for peer tutoring. Page 5 lists the class mean and standard deviation for performance level and slope, and identifies students who meet a discrepancy criterion (lower than 1 standard deviation below the class mean) on both level and slope. These students are chosen for further assessment or intervention.

Across the country, special educators use CBM software to carefully monitor, individualize, and tailor instructional programs. General educators use CBM software to enhance the quality of their instructional programs for all students, including those with disabilities, and to identify students who require additional or alternative educational programs.

RESEARCH PROGRAM ON COMPUTER APPLICATIONS TO CBM

Since 1985, we have been conducting research examining the utility of CBM software. We began by examining effects associated with *electronic management of data that have been collected by hand.* Early discussions (Hasselbring & Hamlett, 1985; Walton, 1986) about the potential for computers to solve the problems associated with ongoing assessment systems had focused on computer applications to manage data. Despite early speculation that data-management systems would improve efficiency, we found that this software *reduced* efficiency. After administering and scoring tests by hand, teachers needed to go to a computer, load software, identify pupils and academic areas to the computer, enter measurement dates and scores, save data, and view or print graphs. By contrast, noncomputer teachers simply located graphs and placed symbols at appropriate places on those graphs (Fuchs et al., 1987). Interestingly, however, although data-management software required more teacher time, teachers were more satisfied with CBM with the computerized data-management condition (Fuchs et al., 1987). Moreover, with the addition of a tutorial routine in the software, which explained the rationale for the computer's instructional decisions, computerized data-management helped teachers understand and comply with CBM data analysis better (Fuchs, Fuchs, &

FIGURE 2. Example of a 5-Page Computer-Generated CBM Class Report in Math Computations and Concepts and Applications

CLASS SUMMARY

Teacher: Mrs. Andersen

Report through 11/21

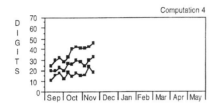

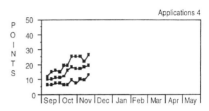

Students to Watch

Peter O'Hara
Fred Wilson
Tami Anderson
Mirian Ahmed
Kenneth Hodges

Most Improved

Javier Perez
DJ Harris
Cesar Hernandez
Jason Katz
Anna Williams

Areas of Improvement: Computation

S1 Subtracting
F1 Add/subtract simple fractions

Areas of Improvement: Applications

GR Grid reading
AP Area and perimeter
Fr   Fractions

Whole Class Instruction: Computation

M3 Multiplying by 2 digits
94% of your students are either COLD or COOL on this skill.

Whole Class Instruction: Applications

CG Charts and graphs
78% of your students are either COLD or COOL on this skill.

Small Group Instruction: Computation

S1 Subtracting
DJ Harris
Joanne Thomas
Tami Anderson

Small Group Instruction: Applications

NC Number concepts
Alicia Johnson
Fred Wilson
Kenneth Hodges
Mirian Ahmed

CLASS SKILLS PROFILE - Computation

Teacher: Mrs. Andersen
Report through 11/21

Name	A1	S1	M1	M2	M3	D1	D2	D3	F1	F2
Alice Porter										
Alicia Johnson										
Anna Williams										
Cesar Hernandez										
Deonte Jones										
DJ Harris										
Ellen Morrison										
Fred Wilson										
Jason Katz										
Javier Perez										
Joanne Thomas										
Joey Kerns										
Karla Stokes										
Kenneth Hodges										
Marilyn Mason										
Mirian Ahmed										
Peter O'Hara										
Tami Anderson										

Legend	A1	S1	M1	M2	M3	D1	D2	D3	F1	F2
☐ COLD. Not tried.	0	2	0	0	0	2	8	9	3	13
▥ COOL. Trying these.	3	4	1	6	17	5	9	5	10	2
▦ WARM. Starting to get it.	4	1	2	2	1	2	0	3	1	2
▪ VERY WARM. Almost have it.	2	2	2	1	0	2	0	1	1	0
■ HOT. You've got it!	9	9	13	9	0	7	1	0	3	1

(Page 2)

RANKED SCORES - Applications

Teacher: Mrs. Andersen
Report through 11/21

Name	Score	Growth
Alice Porter	26	+1.85
Ellen Morrison	24	+1.69
Cesar Hernandez	23	+1.29
Karla Stokes	22	+1.13
Joanne Thomas	22	+1.51
Javier Perez	20	+1.09
Deonte Jones	20	+1.91
Anna Williams	20	+0.87
Joey Kerns	18	+1.57
Jason Katz	18	+0.91
Marilyn Mason	17	+0.55
DJ Harris	16	. . . .
Fred Wilson	15	+0.49
Alicia Johnson	15	+1.09
Peter O'Hara	14	+0.87
Tami Anderson	11	+0.30
Mirian Ahmed	10	+0.96
Kenneth Hodges	5	+0.46

(Page 3)

FIGURE 2 (continued)

Peer Tutoring Assignments
Teacher: Mrs. Andersen
Report through 11/21

M2 Multiplying by 1 digit	First Coach	Second Coach
	■ Marilyn Mason	⊞ Mirian Ahmed
	▫ Joey Kerns	⊞ Deonte Jones
	■ DJ Harris	⊞ Karla Stokes
	⊞ Cesar Hernandez	⊞ Javier Perez
	■ Jason Katz	⊞ Fred Wilson

AP Area and perimeter	First Coach	Second Coach
	■ Ellen Morrison	⊞ Kenneth Hodges
	■ Alice Porter	⊞ Alicia Johnson
	■ Peter O'Hara	⊞ Anna Williams
	■ Joanne Thomas	⊞ Tami Anderson

(Page 4)

CLASS STATISTICS: Computation + Applications
Teacher: Mrs. Andersen
Report through 11/21

Score

Average score	48.9
Standard deviation	13.7
Discrepancy criterion	35.2

Slope

Average Slope	+2.47
Standard deviation	1.13
Discrepancy criterion	+1.34

Students identified with dual discrepancy criterion

	Score	Slope
Kenneth Hodges	16.5	+0.60
Tami Anderson	33.0	+0.72

(Page 5)

Hamlett, 1988). Therefore, although data-management software failed to improve CBM feasibility, we began to understand the computer's capability to assist teachers in other phases of CBM use.

In the next segment of our research program, we investigated the use of computers to *generate, administer, and score* CBM tests. Fuchs et al. (1988) demonstrated that teachers spent substantially less time in measurement when computers automatically collect CBM data. Most teachers, in fact, spend *no* time in administering, scoring, or analyzing assessments. Also, teacher satisfaction with CBM is greater with the data-collection software, and the ease with which teachers can be prepared to use CBM is greatly facilitated. Software can ensure that teachers understand students' assessment profiles, while avoiding large amounts of time to train to criterion in administering, scoring, or analyzing data.

Another persistent CBM implementation problem is teachers' difficulty in translating assessment information into instructional decisions that can be implemented within with the heavy caseloads frequently found today in special and general education. We addressed this problem in three stages: through computerized skills analysis, expert systems, and classwide data analysis and instructional recommendations.

Each CBM administered throughout the year samples all the skills embedded in the year's curriculum. Consequently, two types of CBM information are always available: the total test score as well as an analysis of performance on each curricular skill. Unfortunately, item-by-item analysis is extremely time consuming to complete; and even with time, this analysis cannot be done by hand in an accurate manner. Computers, however, are ideal for completing laborious, intricate item-by-item analyses quickly and accurately.

Therefore, to enhance teachers' use of assessment information for instructional decision making, we developed computerized *skills analysis* to complement CBM total scores. The type and format of the skills analysis differ by academic area (see Fuchs, Fuchs, & Hamlett, 1989 for reading; Fuchs, Fuchs, Hamlett, & Allinder, 1991b for spelling).

We ran an experiment in each academic area to examine how skills analysis might enhance CBM. Findings were robust. Across academic areas, teachers who planned students' programs with skills analyses designed more specific instructional adjustments and effected reliably greater achievement (Fuchs, Fuchs, & Hamlett, 1989; Fuchs, Fuchs, Hamlett, & Allinder, 1991b; Fuchs, Fuchs, Hamlett, & Stecker, 1990).

This increased specificity occurred in teachers more clearly referencing the skills they targeted for remediation (i.e., a better description of what they would teach). Beyond increased specificity about *what* skills to teach, however, a persistent, more intractable problem in teachers' instructional decision making is an inadequate focus on *how* they will teach. When a student has failed to learn a skill, many teachers reteach that skill using the original instructional method (see

Fuchs, Fuchs, Phillips & Simmons, 1993; Putnam, 1987). Although recycling students through the same instructional procedure may work in some cases, a higher level of adaptation occurs when teachers modify not only what they teach students, but also use a different strategy to provide an alternative route for learning (see Corno & Snow, 1986).

Unfortunately, teachers frequently are knowledgeable and comfortable with only one or two instructional methods and, after a student has experienced failure with these methods, teachers often have difficulty identifying additional strategies. Although skills analysis addressed teachers' difficulties in pinpointing which skills to (re)teach, it did not help teachers identify alternative strategies for (re)teaching that material.

In the next phase of our research, therefore, we developed and evaluated the use of *expert systems* to address teachers' difficulty in identifying how to teach students. Expert systems are software programs designed to mimic the thinking of experts. The extent to which these expert systems helped teachers plan better programs varied as a function of content area. In math (Fuchs, Fuchs, Hamlett, & Stecker, 1991), effects were impressive. Expert systems helped teachers design better instructional programs that incorporated a more diverse set of skills and relied on a more varied set of instructional design features. Additionally, students in the expert system CBM group achieved significantly and dramatically better. In reading (Fuchs, Fuchs, Hamlett, & Ferguson, 1992), effects differed for instructional planning and achievement. Expert systems helped teachers plan instructional programs that incorporated more reading skills and utilized more instructional methods. Also, expert system students achieved reliably better than nonexpert system CBM pupils and better than control students on outcome measures involving written retells, a measure that mirrored expert system teachers' greater use of written story grammar instructional activities. On other outcome measures (oral reading fluency and maze), however, both CBM groups achieved comparably well and better than control group students. Results in the area of spelling (Fuchs, Fuchs, Hamlett, & Allinder, 1991a) were least supportive of the expert system. Nonexpert and expert system CBM teachers both effected reliably better achievement outcomes than control teachers; however, achievement of the two CBM groups was not different. Analysis of teachers' instructional plans indicated that expert system teachers relied on practice routines recommended by the expert system to a great extent, but used the expert system's teacher-directed instructional recommendations less frequently. So, expert system advice did not substantially improve decisions formulated by teachers on their own.

Even with technology that could help teachers identify alternative, potentially effective instructional strategies, however, an important feasibility problem with CBM implementation remained: Given CBM's focus on the individual learner, teachers frequently needed to adjust different students' instructional programs, in different ways, at different times. Given the large numbers of students with whom many special and general educators work, an individual focus can be problematic. Therefore, the next step in our research program was to explore how software might help teachers integrate CBM information and instructional recommendations across learners, with the ultimate goal of adapting instructional programs for individual learners.

Fuchs, Fuchs, Hamlett, Bishop, and Bentz (1994) examined the utility of classwide CBM reports and instructional recommendations within general education classrooms that incorporated mainstreamed students with learning disabilities. Results indicated that teachers who employed classwide CBM with instructional recommendations planned more responsively to individual student needs and effected substantially better achievement than teachers who did not use CBM. These effects have held across learning disabled, low-achieving nondisabled, average-achieving, and high-achieving students (Fuchs et al., 1997). Additionally, and importantly, the general educators found the CBM process, which included both measurement and instructional decision making, to be enjoyable and feasible to implement.

IMPLICATIONS

Our 10-year research program on computer applications to CBM permits several conclusions about special education, general education, technology, and assessment. First, in reading, spelling, and math, technology can be used to reduce dramatically the need for teachers to conduct the mechanical tasks associated with assessment, such as test construction and administration, scoring, graphing, and data analysis. Although data-management software, alone, does not increase teacher efficiency, data-generation/collection software, used in combination with data-management software, eliminates almost all teacher time in such tasks. Computers are ideally suited for the completion of this type of repetitive, routine work, and related computer applications for other types of assessment procedures should be developed to help reduce the need for teachers to engage in unchallenging work and to increase their availability for instructional responsibilities.

Second, in addition to completing the mechanical, repetitive aspects of measurement, computers can be used to complete work that human beings would not ordinarily be capable of performing accurately, even with great time expenditures. For example, the computer-generated skills analyses provide a useful supplement to the traditional CBM total test score, allowing teachers to plan more specific instructional programs and to effect greater achievement for their students. Without the use of technology, such skills analyses are not possible. Another example of information that computers can easily generate, which teachers would not be capable of producing reliably, is the class re-ports which aggregate information about many students and automati-cally offer instructional recommendations. Our research again indi-cates that these group reports increase teachers' capacity to plan responsively, even with large groups of students. Researchers and developers should continue to consider how technology can be used not only to save teachers time, but also to enhance the quality of teachers' efforts by completing work that humans would otherwise not be capable of generating.

Third, our work with expert systems and other instructional recom-mendation systems supports their value in helping teachers plan more sound, effective instruction. Nevertheless, our research also suggests that caution is necessary. Use of our expert systems produced differing outcomes, depending on instructional area. Clearly, the availability of computer-generated instructional recommendations, alone, is insuffi-cient to increase teachers' capacity to plan. The nature of the advice and the conditions under which that advice is offered are critical to efficacy. As electronic information and communication systems are developed to increase teachers' access to information, researchers and developers need to consider carefully the quality of the available infor-mation and the conditions under which that information is offered. Also, the efficacy of electronic information and communication sys-tems needs to be evaluated rigorously.

REFERENCES

Corno, L., & Snow, R. E. (1986). Adapting teaching to individual differences among learners. In M. Wittrock (Ed.), *Third handbook of research on teaching* (pp. 605-629). New York: Macmillan.

Deno, S. L. (1985). Curriculum-based measurement: The emerging alternative. *Exceptional Children, 52,* 219-232.

Fuchs, L. S., Deno, S. L., & Mirkin, P. K. (1984). The effects of frequent curriculum-based measurement and evaluation on pedagogy, student achievement, and student awareness of learning. *American Educational Research Journal, 21,* 449-460.

Fuchs, L. S., & Fuchs, D. (1998). Treatment validity: A unifying concept for reconceptualizing the identification of learning disabilities. *Learning Disabilities Research and Practice, 13,* 204-219.

Fuchs, L. S., Fuchs, D., & Hamlett, C. L. (1988). Effects of computer-managed instruction on teachers' implementation of systematic monitoring programs and student achievement. *Journal of Educational Research, 81,* 294-304.

———. (1989). Monitoring reading growth using student recalls: Effects of two teacher feedback systems. *Journal of Educational Research, 83,* 103-111.

Fuchs, L. S., Fuchs, D., Hamlett, C. L., & Allinder, R. M. (1991a). Effects of expert system advice within curriculum-based measurement on teacher planning and student achievement in spelling. *School Psychology Review, 20,* 49-66.

———. (1991b). The contribution of skills analysis to curriculum-based measurement in spelling, *Exceptional Children, 57,* 443-452.

Fuchs, L. S., Fuchs, D., Hamlett, C. L., Bishop, N., & Bentz, J. (1994). Classwide curriculum-based measurement: Helping teachers meet the challenge of student diversity. *Exceptional Children, 60,* 15-24.

Fuchs, L. S., Fuchs, D., Hamlett, C. L., & Ferguson, C. (1992). Effects of expert system consultation within curriculum-based measurement using a reading maze task. *Exceptional Children, 58,* 436-450.

Fuchs, L. S., Fuchs, D., Hamlett, C. L., & Stecker, P. M. (1990). The role of skills analysis in curriculum-based measurement in math. *School Psychology Review, 19,* 6-22.

———. (1991). Effects of curriculum-based measurement and consultation on teacher planning and student achievement in mathematics operations. *American Educational Research Journal, 28,* 617-641.

Fuchs, L. S., Fuchs, D., Hasselbring, T., & Hamlett, C. L. (1987). Using computers with curriculum-based progress monitoring: Effects on teacher efficiency and satisfaction. *Journal of Special Education Technology, 8*(4), 14-27.

Fuchs, L. S, Fuchs, D., Karns, K., Hamlett, C. L., Katzaroff, M., & Dutka, S. (1997). Effects of task-focused goals on low-achieving students with and without learning disabilities. *American Educational Research Journal, 34,* 513-543.

Fuchs, L. S., Fuchs, D., Phillips, N., & Simmons, D. (1993). Contextual variables affecting instructional adaptation. *School Psychology Review, 22,* 722-742.

Fuchs, L. S., Hamlett, C. L., Fuchs, D., Stecker, P. M., & Ferguson, C. (1987). Conducting curriculum-based measurement with computerized data collection: Effects on efficiency and teacher satisfaction. *Journal of Special Education Technology, 9*(2), 73-86.

Hasselbring, T. S., & Hamlett, C. L. (1985). Planning and managing instruction: Computer-based decision making. *Teaching Exceptional Children, 16,* 248-252.

Jones, E. D., & Krouse, J. P. (1988). The effectiveness of data-based instruction by student teachers in classrooms for pupils with mild handicaps. *Teacher Education and Special Education, 11*(1), 9-19.

Putnam, R. T. (1987). Structuring and adjusting content for students: A study of live and simulated tutoring of addition. *American Educational Research Journal, 24,* 13-48.

Walton, W. T. (1986). Educators' response to methods of collecting, storing, and analyzing behavioral data. *Journal of Special Education Technology, 7,* 50-55.

Wesson, C. L. (1991). Curriculum-based measurement and two models of follow-up consultation. *Exceptional Children, 57,* 246-257.

Wesson, C. L., King, R. P., & Deno, S. L. (1984). Direct and frequent measurement: If it's so good for us, why don't we use it? *Learning Disability Quarterly, 7*(1), 45-48.

Constructivism and the Role of Skills in Mathematics Instruction for Academically At-Risk Secondary Students

John Woodward

University of Puget Sound

SUMMARY. Instructional uses of technology in special education have evolved considerably over the last two decades. Many researchers have moved away from stand alone uses (e.g., computer assisted instruction) toward an array of different technologies that serve as tools in complex learning environments. A change in thinking about teaching and learning has also occurred, as researchers have moved away from didactic instructional methods to constructivist approaches. Yet constructivism remains problematic for many in the field, in part because of the traditional emphasis on skills in day-to-day instruction. This article describes how skills instruction can be an important feature of constructivism for teaching special education students. *[Article copies available for a fee from The Haworth Document Delivery Service: 1-800-342-9678. E-mail address: <getinfo@haworthpressinc.com> Website: <http://www.HaworthPress.com>]*

KEYWORDS. Constructivism, mathematics instruction, at-risk students, computers

Two decades ago, a number of visionaries like Bork (1981) and Papert (1980) proclaimed that computers would "revolutionize" learn-

Address correspondence to: Dr. John Woodward, School of Education, The University of Puget Sound, 1500 North Warner, Tacoma, WA 98416-0220.

[Haworth co-indexing entry note]: "Constructivism and the Role of Skills in Mathematics Instruction for Academically At-Risk Secondary Students." Woodward, John. Co-published simultaneously in *Special Services in the Schools* (The Haworth Press, Inc.) Vol. 17, No. 1/2, 2001, pp. 15-31; and: *Computers in the Delivery of Special Education and Related Services: Developing Collaborative and Individualized Learning Environments* (ed: Louis J. Kruger) The Haworth Press, Inc., 2001, pp. 15-31. Single or multiple copies of this article are available for a fee from The Haworth Document Delivery Service [1-800-342-9678, 9:00 a.m. - 5:00 p.m. (EST). E-mail address: getinfo@haworthpressinc.com].

15

ing. In fact, public schools during the 1980s spent approximately $2 billion for microcomputers in pursuit of this revolution, and acquisitions in special education alone grew more than 330% from 1983 to 1985 (Blaschke, 1985). Many educators, from university researchers to public school teachers, felt that a substantive infusion of technology into our schools would make learning far more productive and meaningful. In this sense, they were following what Cuban (1993) was later to characterize as the "technophile's vision" of computer-based education. Schools were to become, "total settings that have a critical mass of machines, software, and like-minded people who are serious users of technology" (p. 192).

In special education, the technophile's vision had its own unique characteristics. While there was an equal interest in the scale of innovation (e.g., the critical mass of computers needed to serve children, the amount of time students would spend on computers), the proposed uses were less lofty than some, like Papert (1980), had articulated. Instead of spending time exploring microworlds and programming in LOGO, special educators felt that computers could solve a number of relatively mundane tasks facing the practitioner (Woodward & Rieth, 1997). Computer programs could help teachers reliably identify students who were eligible for services, track progress toward IEP goals, *and* augment instruction. As for this latter use, computers could provide the kind of systematic practice that students with disabilities needed in order to master basic skills. Special educators often envisioned the instructional use of computers as Computer Assisted Instruction (CAI). Consequently, much of the research on computer technology focused on drill and practice and low-level tutorial programs.

Trends in technology-based instruction over the last decade indicate that both the technophile and CAI vision are changing (Woodward & Rieth, 1997). This is occurring for a number of important reasons, the first of which has to do with the gap between what researchers identified as high quality software and what was actually available to practitioners. In the late 1980s, many special education technologists studied the specific dimensions of CAI in the attempt to determine what characteristics or instructional design features (see Woodward et al., 1986) could optimize CAI programs. Although this body of research validated the role of specific forms of feedback, explicit strategies, and distributed practice, far too few of these "optimized" basic skills programs were successfully marketed to practitioners. Most CAI programs that were used in experimental studies remained in some proto-typic form.

Yet even if these programs were to reach practitioners, researchers were discovering naturalistic factors that tended to work against the effective use of CAI programs. Far too many students in our public schools had difficulty accessing computers for the 20 to 30 minutes per day needed to improve basic skills. Case study research (MacArthur & Malouf, 1991) also revealed that teachers selected CAI programs for their motivational features and not necessarily their instructional capabilities. Finally, as Woodward (1993) suggests in his review of technology-based programs, teachers seemed uninterested in such comprehensive, "day-in and day-out" approaches to education. Few wanted to spend their days monitoring students in computer labs or play the next programmed segment of a videodisc lesson. Other researchers (Cuban, 1993; Huberman, 1993) echo this sentiment, suggesting that teachers are generally reluctant to give up the intimacy of teacher-student contacts during instruction.

A third force that has contributed to the demise of CAI has been the influence of cognitive psychology on the field. This was first apparent in early efforts to model student understanding on highly procedural tasks such as subtraction (Woodward & Howard, 1994) and multiplication (Gerber, Semmel, & Semmel, 1994). What quickly followed was an interest by many in constructivist approaches to education. Special education technologists explored the use of computers as tools in complex instructional environments. The tools varied from common but highly useful technologies like hand calculators to powerful multimedia configurations that include scanners, digital cameras, and state-of-the-art desktop computers. These uses, which were also taking hold among educational technologists outside the field of special education, relegated these different technologies to the role of a compensatory aid for problem solving, a presentational medium, or a vehicle for stimulating or refining an issue. Recent examples of special education technology research include calculators as tools that replace excessive computational practice (Woodward, Baxter, & Robinson, in press), videodiscs for complex mathematical problem solving (Bottge & Hasselbring, 1993; Cognition and Technology Group at Vanderbilt University, 1997), microcomputers for thematic projects in literature (Zorfass & Copel, 1995), and multimedia systems that help students develop argumentative writing in social studies (Feretti & Okolo, 1996).

To be sure, many special education technologists have moved from away from CAI and, more generally, an exclusive focus on skills-based instruction. However, it would be a serious misstatement to suggest that the field has embraced constructivism or even found consensus on what constitute appropriate constructivist practices. In fact, coming to terms with constructivism *is* one of the major issues in intervention research in our field today, particularly as researchers grapple with the role of skills in any kind of complex learning. The confusion over the balance between skills and what many perceived as a new form of student-directed learning is apparent in the recent intervention literature.

For example, the special issue of *Journal of Special Education* (summer, 1994) on constructivism contains position papers that offer clearly diverse views of the topic. Harris and Graham (1994) review different paradigms of constructivism in the effort to demonstrate its complexity, and to show how skill development is *and should be* a major concern in any content area instruction. Mercer, Jordan, and Miller (1994) cautiously entertain the potential of some forms of constructivism, but contend that its use, particularly in mathematics, must be first validated by rigorous empirical research. Dixon and Carnine (1994) offer a more radical response to constructivism, dismissing it along with other learning theories as ideologies.

Subsequent writings not only show a continued struggle with various interpretations of constructivism, but awkward attempts to merge constructivist notions with direct instruction pedagogy. Gersten and Baker's (1998) recent attempt to fuse situated cognition with direct instruction concludes with the suggestion that teachers can be taught to switch back and forth from one paradigm to the other as they teach skills in problem solving contexts. Tarver's (1996) takes this kind of thinking a step further by claiming that the direct instruction principles (e.g., explicit, step-by-step strategies; curricular materials that are broken into small steps; extensive practice with considerable teacher feedback) used to develop commercial programs such as Reading Mastery ™, Corrective Reading ™, and Connecting Mathematics Concepts ™, exemplify "true" constructivist principles. For Tarver, the mainstream notions of constructivism are lamentably equivalent to discovery learning and thus, entirely inappropriate for teaching students with disabilities.

The field's conflicted views of constructivism are significant and not easily resolved. Although this article will do little to answer questions at the rhetorical or theoretical level, it does provide an extended example of how constructivism and the "problem of skills" can be addressed in a conceptually coherent way. What I will argue is that one needs a different sense of skill instruction than what commonly appears in the special education literature. Part of the field's confusion, it seems, involves the assumption that if skills need to be taught, the only way to teach them is through well-established approaches such as direct instruction. There are few opportunities for open-ended inquiry or student-guided learning. This assumption leads quickly and obviously to theoretical conflicts, as the literature just reviewed suggests.

One way out of this confusion is to see how skill instruction naturally emanates from a social constructivist view of teaching and learning. That is, an individual student's learning occurs in a rich social context (Lave & Wenger, 1991; Palincsar, 1998). Conjecture and collective inquiry are defining features of a classroom community. Student's take an increasingly active role in acquiring new knowledge through strategies that were initially modeled by the teacher. However, unlike the extreme views of constructivism that appear in the special education literature (e.g., students are left to "learn on their own" in ways reminiscent of discovery learning), the teacher continues to play a critical role in framing problems, clarifying issues as they arise, continually prodding students to extend their reasoning, and, at times, "showing how." This latter characteristic is essential to the apprenticeship dimensions of social constructivism. As apprentices, students need to be shown how to perform certain tasks or practice specific skills. It is hoped that the extended description that follows later in this article will articulate how skills instruction–"showing how"–is compatible with the social constructivist view of teaching.

THE WORKPLACE LITERACY PROJECT

Our most recently completed work in constructivist approaches to education involves the Workplace Literacy Project. The purpose of this project was to articulate a type of instruction that better prepares students with learning disabilities for work in a rapidly changing world. Throughout the 1990s, seemingly countless policy documents and mainstream publications (e.g., Greider, 1997; Reich, 1991) have detailed the characteristics that a new kind of worker–a knowledge worker–will need in an information economy. If one is to be employed at a level beyond minimum wages, individuals will need to have much more than a knowledge of basic skills, even though this is a common focus of instruction for secondary students with learning disabilities. Documents such as *What Work Requires of Schools* (US Department of Labor, 1991) clearly articulate how successful workers in the future will need to demonstrate a capacity for higher order thinking, a proficiency in interpersonal skills, and conversance in a range of common, technological tools.

Throughout the project, researchers worked with remedial and special education math teachers to create classroom environments where students took a much more active role in their learning. At times, teachers initially modeled new ways of thinking and acting. However, teachers quickly moved from this kind of teaching to periods of sustained classroom dialogue and small group, cooperative learning. In addition to instruction that focused on the conceptual dimensions of core middle school mathematics topics, students worked on problems that spanned several days. The problems often integrated their mathematical investigations with written and oral communication. Calculators, spreadsheets, and word processors were typically available as tools for problem solving and communication.

What follows is a detailed example of instruction and student learning during the Workplace Literacy Project. The example focuses on the mathematics component of the project because this is a rich arena for describing the meaning of skills and their role in constructivist practice. The example shows how skills and different types of knowledge are interrelated. I begin by contrasting the approach used in the project with traditional special education practices as well as a recent attempt in special education to apply constructivist principles in mathematics for students with learning disabilities.

Integrating Different Kinds of Mathematical Knowledge

Traditional mathematics instruction in special education largely focuses on declarative and procedural knowledge (i.e., factual and "how to" knowledge). Students are taught math facts, and they apply them procedurally as they work computational algorithms for basic operations such as subtraction or division. Learning to solve simple, "one step" word problems by looking for key words (e.g., "per means to multiply") and then solving the problem using the relevant algorithm is another kind of procedural knowledge. As Hasselbring and his colleagues (Bottge & Hasselbring, 1993; Cognition and Technology Group at Vanderbilt University, 1997; Hasselbring, 1994) note, rarely is this kind of knowledge linked to the use of conditional knowledge (i.e., "when to apply") where students engage in authentic, highly contextualized problem solving.

Bottge and Hasselbring's (1993) study of mathematical problem solving demonstrated the potential of highly contextualized or "anchored" instruction. After secondary students with learning disabilities had learned fractions in a task analytic, direct instruction manner, students in the comparison group continued to solve problems using set procedures for identifying extraneous information and key words. Experimental students, in contrast, were shown real world problems through video vignettes. They discussed these problems by means of a teacher-guided discussion. The teacher initially helped students break down the problems into manageable units of information, posed different solution strategies, and asked "what if?" questions which helped students focus on how the problem would have been different given new information. Gradually, these responsibilities were turned over to the students.

Bottge and Hasselbring found significant differences favoring the experimental group, who received "anchored instruction." However, the study was problematic insofar as it was grounded in conflicting theoretical orientations. The experimental students spent several weeks in a didactic, skills-based program *before* the anchored problem solving. Although this structure was understandable given the purpose and design of the study, it also exemplified the confusion that exists about skills instruction for special education students. Means and Knapp (1991), among others, have been highly critical of the linear format of this kind of instruction, where students initially master discrete, isolated skills without a more global sense of why these skills are important or where they apply.

A further problem with the skills stage of the Bottge and Hasselbring study was that by relying on curriculum that was developed in accordance with a highly task analytic approach, many of the procedural skills (e.g., extended practice adding unusual fractions such as $2/7$ and $3/11$ by hand) and tasks were of little relevance to the subsequent problem solving. In other words, what followed logically as an important skill in a task analytic curriculum was not useful in another one. This would have been particularly apparent if tools such as calculators had been part of the intervention.

Linking intuitive, concrete, and conceptual knowledge. When we began our Workplace Literacy efforts, we individually interviewed several students about their impressions of mathematics as well as their competence in several topic areas such as rational numbers. Jasmine was a talkative and pleasant eighth grade girl who had had several years of remedial math. In fact, she had just finished a highly structured skills program like the one used in the Bottge and Hasselbring (1993) study. When she was asked if she would rather work the problem $3.73 \times .14$ by hand or with a calculator, she immediately said that she would use a calculator because, "I still get a little confused with my times." She was also asked if she could convert the fractional representation of 2/5 into a decimal. She proceeded confidently and quickly, producing what she thought was the right answer. She wrote 10.000 and then, without prompting, added 10.00%.

Unfortunately, Jasmine multiplied the numerator and denominator to derive her first answer. It should also be mentioned that she was not asked to write the problem in a percent form. When the interviewer explained the nature of her error, she was asked to work on a second problem (this time, the pictorial representation of two-thirds) with a calculator. She had no difficulties with this problem and successfully rounded the number to the 100th place in a rapid and routine manner. Like many other students who we interviewed, Jasmine carries a calculator in her backpack every day.

Jasmine's experiences as part of the Workplace Literacy Project were markedly different from what she had learned before in other low track math classes at Marcus Middle School. Along with her other classmates, Jasmine began investigating rational numbers (fractions and decimals, specifically) in two ways. First, Dan Wilson, a pseudonym for the teacher in our project, selected an array of visual representations to work through and discuss. Wilson operated on the premise that these students had an intuitive knowledge of fractions as well as fragmented procedural and declarative knowledge from their previous years of traditional, skills-based teaching. Consequently, Wilson did not "begin at the beginning," but provoked a discussion of how quantities can be partitioned. During several lessons, he used fraction bars, pie diagrams, "egg crate" drawings, and measuring cups to do this. An example of these representations and their equivalence can be seen in Figure 1.

Students discussed various representations, and Wilson was quick to promote further discussion as student misconceptions or confusion arose in class. For example, when students were working through the concept of equivalent fractions, Jasmine had difficulty visualizing how 4/12 of an egg crate drawing and 1/3 of the same drawing were the same. Rather than telling Jasmine the answer or "proving it" by reducing 4/12 to 1/3, Wilson asked his students work on an explanation. After 10 minutes in small groups, several students shared their solutions. Cyndi, another student in the class, used the overhead projector, and started by referring to fraction bars. By juxtaposing two different fraction bars, Cyndi showed how the area they covered was the same. Wilson complemented Cyndi's explanation by drawing the fraction bars on the overhead one atop the other, and then coloring in the same areas. He prodded Cyndi to follow this by doing the same with two egg crate figures. Cyndi drew one crate with 12 squares and the other as just an outline of the crate with 3 vertical lines. The class talked through the comparison of the two figures, again emphasizing the equivalence of the two areas. Wilson continued to probe student understanding, occasionally drawing attention to the role that "dividing up" or partitioning played in fractions. As a way of summarizing the discussion, he also noted that the same concept applies to decimals.

Rather than waiting until his students had "completed" their conceptual understanding of fractions, Wilson introduced what appeared to be a simple problem that students were to solve using paper, pencil,

FIGURE 1. Multiple Representations Used to Visualize Fractions

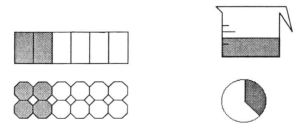

and "fraction calculators" (i.e., inexpensive calculators that show fractions in their canonical or traditional form in the LCD display). Wilson gave each student a worksheet with a large circle divided into 24 slices or segments. He asked the students to use a piece of lined paper to first list the main things they did every day by category and the number of hours for each categorical activity (e.g., eating, sleeping, going to school). He instructed students to round each activity to the hour. Once students compiled 24 hours worth of activities, they colored and labeled the appropriate portion of the circle (e.g., if they watched TV for 3 hours every day, then they colored three segments and labeled this colored section of the circle).

Wilson subsequently led the class in a discussion of the numbers that represented the different colored section. Students were quick to pick up on the pattern (e.g., Jasmine watched TV for 3/24 of the day, slept for 9/24, was in school 8/24, and ate and did other things 4/24 of the day). Noting that 9/24 was an "awkward fraction," Wilson asked them to use their fraction calculators to reduce these numbers where possible (e.g., 3/24 simplified to 1/8 by first entering 3/24 and then pressing the SIMP button). Students finished the lesson by computing the number of hours per school week they spent on their main activities and contrasted these proportions to what they did on the weekends. Wilson used the contrast between the typical day during the week and weekend to discuss changes in proportion for the same activity, consistently asking which fraction was greater. All of his students could see intuitively the greater proportion of time they spent watching TV on the weekends.

Constructivist foundations of Wilson's lessons. This segment from Wilson's early instruction in fractions not only highlights constructivist pedagogical principles at work, but it suggests specific assumptions Wilson has made making mathematics meaningful to secondary remedial learners and those with learning disabilities. Wilson is well aware that these students have been "taught" fractions before. Most likely, it has been through a highly symbolic approach, one that is likely to have been similar to the preskill instruction phase of the Bottge and Hasselbring (1993) study. This kind of approach had clearly failed, as Jasmine's interview described earlier suggests.

Wilson's extensive visual and conceptual treatment of fractions, then, reflects a highly intentional effort at breaking a pattern of what students often perceive as aimless symbol manipulation. His concern is to connect a simple intuitive understanding of fractions as a single ratio to more complex and abstract representations. This approach is consistent with a number of mathematics researchers who endorse the role of multiple visual representations in fractions (Silver, 1986) as well as the role of teacher-guided discussions and explorations (Hiebert & Carpenter, 1992).

This brief vignette of Wilson's introductory instruction also reveals a concern for connecting conceptual understanding with everyday events. Wilson is careful to draw on readily available mental models as a basis for applying conceptual knowledge rather than solely relying on complex, ill-defined problems that take a considerable period of time to develop and understand. Even though Wilson asks students to work on some problems that span several days or even a week, this is just one type of problem solving activity, and it has to be tempered by his sense of the curriculum, student understanding, and where he intends to guide his students next. I will return to this point shortly when I discuss how Wilson uses fractions later in the year in more complex problem solving contexts.

Wilson's introductory lessons also involve the discretionary use of a simple technology–the fraction calculator. This tool, which effectively supersedes the need to compute complicated problems by hand (e.g., adding 2/7 and 4/9), helps reinforce the notion that the use of specific tools and strategies are shaped by the context. One of Wilson's main goals is to get students to differentiate when to use paper and pencil, calculators, and/or mental strategies when they do mathematics. Traditional approaches tend to promote an over-reliance on paper and pencil, hand computational strategies.

The role of skills. The content that is described in the forgoing example is consistent with a number of conceptually guided approaches to reform mathematics instruction. Arguably, one reason for these kinds of descriptions is to highlight new forms of pedagogy and the active role of students in their own learning. For those reasons and undoubtedly others, skill instruction is under-described.

Yet trying to infuse a traditional, direct instruction approach to the skills that underlie Wilson's instruction would be a mistake. This is not only because direct instruction's theoretical orientation runs counter to constructivism, but because skills in this context have a substantively different meaning than they do when direct instruction approaches are used to teach mathematics to special education students.

Throughout the year, as Wilson works from fractions to decimals and percents, he consistently reviewed specific skills that supported conceptual understanding and problem solving in rational numbers. On an almost daily basis, students compared the relative values of fractions and, at a later point, decimals (e.g., 7/8 is greater than 3/4, "give me a decimal slightly smaller than .56"). Students also practiced rounding decimals to "anchor decimals" like 1/3, 3/8, and 3/4 (e.g., .29 is about .33 which is 1/3).

All of this occurred briefly as regular warm-up exercises or as a break from group discussion or problem solving. Wilson always made a point of connecting this kind of skills practice to other contexts where, for example, his students were using calculators or spreadsheets and came up with large decimal numbers that they couldn't interpret.

Finally, traditional skill practice in fractions such as converting unlike denominators to common denominators and then adding or subtracting was done in a conceptually-guided manner. For example, Wilson's students learned how to perform this kind of task on relatively simple fractions (e.g., $3/5 - 1/10$). However, first they estimated the answer using a visual representation, and then Wilson asked them to explain what they were doing conceptually. For more complex problems (e.g., 5/12 + 3/8), they worked backward from an answer they first derive on their fraction calculators. Once they found the answer and, by default, the common denominator, they used equivalence to finish the exercise. A partially completed portion of a student worksheet problem is shown in Figure 2.

It should be apparent that skill practice like this is a necessary component of the surrounding instruction. The practice occurs briefly, purposefully, and with the wider uses of the skills always apparent. In fact, Wilson makes a special point to make the connection of these

FIGURE 2. Solving Fractions by "Working Backwards"

$$\frac{5}{12} \quad - \quad = \quad \frac{}{24}$$

$$+ \quad \frac{3}{8} \quad \frac{3}{3} \quad = \quad \frac{}{24}$$

$$\frac{19}{24}$$

skills to how they are applied in other contexts explicit, either through prodding students about the link or making the connection himself.

Recursive review. Task analytic conceptions of instruction move students from a beginning point through stages of mastery to the end of a topic before they begin a new topic. For example, students learn all about fractions, then they effectively abandon this topic once they begin learning about decimals. In addition to the highly procedural focus that often accompanies this kind of instruction, students rarely see how a topic like fractions applies and is embedded in other, less obvious contexts.

Kieren (1993) proposes that students need to learn difficult concepts like rational numbers recursively. That is, students need to learn these concepts from symbolic, visual, and intuitive frameworks. Wilson's introductory lessons on fractions exemplify this kind of linkage. However, a further step, one that builds on other intuitive knowledge, is the kind of anchored instruction activities which researchers like Hasselbring and his colleagues at Vanderbilt University (Cognition and Technology Group at Vanderbilt University, 1993; Hasselbring, 1994) have investigated. Anchored problem solving requires students to investigate problems in a much more detailed and naturalistic way than what Wilson required of his students when they analyzed their daily activities using a pie diagram.

Wilson uses a variety of problems that are rooted in the middle school as a way of anchoring student understanding and, in the context of the Workplace Literacy Project, connects this understanding to the world of work. An example of linking school-based problems to work was the french fries lesson. One week, Wilson asks his students to buy french fries from the school cafeteria and bring them to their fifth period class. The students weighed, measured, and eventually ate all of their fries after they had recorded the data. After entering the data into a spreadsheet the next day, students calculated the overall mean length and weight of their fries. They also examined the systematic relationship between those baskets with greater numbers of fries below the mean and baskets with a greater overall number of fries when the weights of the baskets were approximately equal. In some baskets, students found that 7 of the 20 baskets–or approximately 1/3 when they rounded–had fries that measured less than the overall mean. Similar analyses, including line graphs, were conducted based on the weight of each basket.

As an anchored, school-based problem, students were able to understand the context of this problem intuitively because of its intimate connection to their everyday lives. However, Wilson posed the following question after students determined that there was a considerable fluctuation in the weight and number of french fries in baskets sold in the school cafeteria. "What if McDonald's™ added just a few extra fries to every one of its large basket of fries? Would it make any difference?"

During the next two days, Wilson provided sample baskets of large fries from McDonald's for analysis. The class determined that each large basket contained a mean of 70 fries, and they agreed that five extra fries would be a reasonable definition of "a few extra." After further discussion, students learned that giving away 5 out of 70 fries (or 5/70 which equalled 1/14) meant that every 15th basket of fries would be free. Students estimated that each basket cost $1.09, and that for the purposes of this problem, McDonald's sold 300,000 baskets of fries worldwide on a daily basis. Using the spreadsheet to model this problem and perform the computations, they determined that adding "just a few extra fries" would result in about a $22,000 loss of revenue each day.

This kind of anchored activity is important for several reasons. First, it links an intuitive and everyday issue (i.e., fries in the cafeteria) to a problem in the world of work that is comprehensible. All of Wilson's students had eaten fries from McDonald's. In fact, the discussion of the potential revenue loss led several students to speculate that the fries at McDonald's were cut and packaged in a special way so as to prevent this kind of surplus.

What makes these kinds of activities equally important is that readily available mental models of the problem make it easier for students to concentrate on the complex interplay of mathematics. The spreadsheet representation of the McDonald's problem called for the use of fractions and decimals, multiplication and division, and the conversion of fields with large decimal numbers to currency values (e.g., 11.135656 to $11.14). Working through a problem like this—what the National Council of Teachers of Mathematics encourages a "working with data"—requires detailed attention. It is also on these occasions that students like Jasmine see the meaningful connections of what they've been learning for years to actual problems.

CONCLUDING REMARKS

The Workforce Literacy Project attempted to combine reform mathematics instruction with varying kinds of problem solving activities. The Project is guided by constructivist pedagogy as well as the intention to blend conceptually-oriented instruction with application problems that are embedded in the student's world and, on other occasions, the world of work. The latter problems represent the kind of anchored instruction activities that have an increasing prominence in special education technology research (see Woodward & Rieth, 1997). Our interpretation of constructivist practice for students with learning disabilities also appropriates sufficient room for skill development. We believe that the kind of skill development described in the example above is consistent with socio-cultural approaches to learning, particularly where the metaphor of apprenticeship is employed (Lave & Wenger, 1991; Rogoff, 1990). Our view of skill instruction does not emanate from a traditional direct instruction orientation, and it does not require teachers to continually "switch hats" as they move from skills to problem solving. Rather, skills are a natural and logical component of the broader goals teachers pursue as they attempt to guide students toward a deeper understanding of mathematics and how it is central to the current and future world of work.

REFERENCES

Blaschke, C. (1985). Technology trends in special education. *T.H.E. Journal, 14*(2), 73-77.

Bork, A. (1981). Educational technology and the future. *Journal of Educational Technology Systems, 10*(1), 3-19.

Bottge, B., & Hasselbring, T. (1993). A comparison of two approaches for teaching complex, authentic mathematics problems to adolescents in remedial math classes. *Exceptional Children, 59*(6), 545-556.

Cognition and Technology Group at Vanderbilt University (1997). Complex mathematical problem solving by individuals and dyads. *Cognition and Instruction, 15*(4), 435-84.

Cognition and Technology Group at Vanderbilt University (1993). Integrated media: Toward a theoretical framework for utilizing their potential. *Journal of Special Education Technology., 12*(2), 71-85.

Cuban, L. (1993). The computer meets the classroom: Classroom wins. *Teacher College Record, 95*(2), 184-210.

Dixon, R., & Carnine, D. (1994). Ideologies, practices, and their implications for special education. *The Journal of Special Education, 28*(3), 356-367.

Ferretti, R., & Okolo, C. (1996). Authenticity in learning: Multimedia design projects in the social studies for students with disabilities. *Journal of Learning Disabilities, 29*(5), 450-60.

Gerber, M., Semmel, D., & Semmel, M. (1994). Computer-based dynamic assessment of multidigit multiplication. *Exceptional Children, 61*(2), 114-125.

Gersten, R., & Baker, S. (1998). Real world use of scientific concepts: Integrating situated cognition with explicit instruction. *Exceptional Children, 65*(1), 23-36.

Greider, W. (1997). *One world ready or not: The manic logic of global capitalism.* New York: Simon & Schuster.

Harris, K., & Graham, S. (1994). Constructivism: Principles, paradigms, and integration. *The Journal of Special Education, 28*(3), 233-247.

Hasselbring, T. (1994). Using media for developing mental models and anchoring instruction. *American Annals of the Deaf, 139,* 36-44.

Hiebert, J., & Carpenter, T. (1992). Learning and teaching with understanding. In D. Grouws (Ed.), *Handbook of research on mathematics research and teaching* (pp. 65-100). New York: MacMillan.

Huberman, M. (1993). The model of the independent artisan in teachers' professional relations. In J. Little & M. McLaughlin (Eds.), *Teachers' work* (pp. 11-50). New York: Teachers' College Press.

Kieren, T. (1993). Rational and fractional numbers: From quotient fields to recursive understanding. In T. Carpenter, E. Fennema, & T. Romberg (Eds.), *Rational numbers: An integration of research.* Hillsdale, NJ: LEA.

Lave, J., & Wenger, E. (1991). *Situated learning: Legitimate peripheral participation.* New York: Cambridge University Press.

MacArthur, C., & Malouf, D. (1991). Teachers' beliefs, plans, and decisions about computer-based instruction. *Journal of Special Education, 25*(5), 44-72.

Means, B., & Knapp, M. (1991). Introduction. In B. Means, C. Chelemer, & M. Knapp (Eds.), *Teaching advanced skills to at-risk students: Views from research and practice* (pp. 1-26). San Francisco: Jossey-Bass Publishers.

Mercer, C., Jordan, L., & Miller, S. (1994). Implications of constructivism for teaching math to students with moderate to mild disabilities. *The Journal of Special Education, 28*(3), 290-306.

Palincsar, A. (1998). Social constructivist perspectives on teaching and learning. In J. Spence, J. Darley, and D. Foss (Eds.), *Annual review of psychology vol. 49,* (pp. 345-75). Palo Alto, CA: Annual Reviews.

Papert, S. (1980). *Mindstorms.* New York: Basic Books.

Reich, R. (1991). *The wealth of nations.* New York: Knopf.

Rogoff, B. (1990). *Apprenticeship in thinking: Cognitive development in social context.* New York: Oxford University Press.

Silver, E. (1986). Using conceptual and procedural knowledge. In J. Hiebert (Ed.), *Conceptual and procedural knowledge: The case of mathematics* (pp. 181-198). Hillsdale, NJ: LEA.

Tarver, S. (1996). Direct instruction. In W. Stainback & S. Stainback (Eds.), *Controversial issues confronting special education: Divergent perspectives* (pp. 143-152). Needham Heights, MA: Allyn & Bacon.

US Department of Labor (1991). *What Work Requires of Schools.* Washington, DC: Author. (ERIC Document Reproduction Service No. ED 332054)

Woodward, J. (1993). The technology of technology-based instruction: Comments on the research, development, and dissemination perspective of educational innovation. *Education and Treatment of Children, 16*(4), 345-360.

Woodward, J., Carnine, D., Gersten, R., Gleason, M., Johnson, G., & Collins, M. (1986). Applying instructional design principles to CAI for mildly handicapped students: Four recently conducted studies. *Journal of Special Education Technology, 8*(1), 13-26.

Woodward, J., & Howard, L. (1994). The misconceptions of youth: Errors and their mathematical meaning. *Exceptional Children, 61*(2), 126-136.

Woodward, J., & Rieth, H. (1997). An historical review of technology research in special education. *Review of Educational Research, 67*(4), 503-536.

Zorfass, J., & Copel, H. (1995). The I-Search: Guiding students toward relevant research. *Educational Leadership, 53*(1), 48-51.

Enabling Constructivist Teaching
Through Telementoring

D. Kevin O'Neill

University of Toronto (OISE/UT)

SUMMARY. On-line mentoring is a relatively new way to support students and teachers in the pursuit of ambitious constructivist learning. Using examples from classroom practice, this paper describes such "telementoring" relationships, and how they differ from traditional mentoring, apprenticeship and tutoring. The design and use of a telementored curriculum unit in middle school science is then discussed, and a set of general guidelines is provided to aid teachers and administrators in designing and carrying out their own telementoring initiatives. *[Article copies available for a fee from The Haworth Document Delivery Service: 1-800-342-9678. E-mail address: <getinfo@haworthpressinc.com> Website: <http://www.HaworthPress. com>]*

KEYWORDS. Mentoring, Internet, constructivism, science learning

Address correspondence to: Dr. D. Kevin O'Neill, Research Associate, 562 LRDC, University of Pittsburgh, 3939 O'Hara Street, Pittsburgh, PA 15260.

The author wishes to acknowledge Rory Wagner, Judith LaChance-Whitcomb, and their 1995/96 classes who were invaluable collaborators in this work. He gratefully acknowledges the financial support of the National Science Foundation, under grant #RED-945729, and the Illinois State Board of Education. This program of research continues in collaboration with the CSILE/Knowledge-Building team at the Ontario Institute for Studies in Education of the University of Toronto, with support from the James S. McDonnell Foundation, the Natural Sciences and Engineering Research Council of Canada, and the Office of Learning Technologies, Human Resources Development Canada.

[Haworth co-indexing entry note]: "Enabling Constructivist Teaching Through Telementoring." O'Neill, D. Kevin. Co-published simultaneously in *Special Services in the Schools* (The Haworth Press, Inc.) Vol. 17, No. 1/2, 2001, pp. 33-58; and: *Computers in the Delivery of Special Education and Related Services: Developing Collaborative and Individualized Learning Environments* (ed: Louis J. Kruger) The Haworth Press, Inc., 2001, pp. 33-58. Single or multiple copies of this article are available for a fee from The Haworth Document Delivery Service [1-800-342-9678, 9:00 a.m. - 5:00 p.m. (EST). E-mail address: getinfo@haworthpressinc.com].

INTRODUCTION

All over North America, a remarkable thing is happening. School systems whose budgets are already strained are choosing to invest scarce dollars in computing and network technologies. Often driven by a faith that technical proficiency will lead to better employment for their students, school officials are responding to a swell of public urgency to bring the Internet into every student's life (Robertson, 1998).

One popular orienting metaphor for much of this hurried activity is that of the Internet as a "global library." Unfortunately, the global library metaphor is a poor tool for thinking about how the Internet might foster more independent, constructivist learning. Because the library metaphor focuses attention on the prepared content that networks make available, rather than the value of students' own ideas and the refinement of those ideas (cf. Scardamalia & Bereiter, 1997), it de-emphasizes students' role as active constructors of knowledge. Instead of helping realize the opportunities that new technologies present to approach educational problems in better ways (Soloway & Norris, 1998), the library metaphor leads us to shoehorn technology into familiar roles. The highly-publicized initiative to replace textbooks with laptops in Texas schools (Chapman, 1998) may take this idea to its most absurd extreme.

ENGAGING ADULT COMMUNITIES OF PRACTICE ON THE NET

Thankfully, the global library is not the only metaphor available to guide educators' thinking about how the Internet might serve students' diverse needs. We can also think of the Internet as a *bridge* that makes possible, for the first time, dialogue between students in school and adults in the workplace that is frequent enough, inexpensive enough, and routine enough to enrich curricula deeply. In place of the brief and isolated encounters that students have with adults during field trips and career days, the Internet may allow students' academic work to overlap with the work of adults in ways that initiate them into communities of discourse and practice (Lave & Wenger, 1991) which physical distance and the conflicting schedules of school and work have traditionally kept from them. The ultimate extension of this idea is a network-based "knowledge society" (Scardamalia & Bereiter, 1996) in which students and adults in a variety of fields participate together in learning.

Realizing these opportunities is not so straightforward that it can be done well on the first try. It requires continued experimentation, and the freedom to refine programs for individual schools and clientele. In this article I will review a program of research and development that I have been pursuing for the past five years in cooperation with a handful of teachers in both suburban and urban schools (O'Neill & Gomez, 1994; O'Neill & Gomez, 1998; O'Neill, Wagner & Gomez, 1996). This work revolves around what Wighton (1993) called "telementoring," or mentoring using telecommunications technology.

TRADITIONAL MENTORING

While the idea of mentoring dates back to Homer, today we use the term to describe a wide variety of both pre-arranged and spontaneous relationships in school and business communities (Jacobi, 1991; Kram, 1985; Phillips-Jones, 1982). While researchers differ on precise definitions, "mentoring" generally denotes a supportive relationship between an older, more experienced person and a younger protégé that serves to initiate her into a new profession, organization, or stage in life. Mentoring enthusiasts are also generally sympathetic with the Vygotskyan view that the learning of any complex subject-matter or practice is the result of voices encountering each other and becoming internalized by learners (Vygotsky, 1978).

In the field of education, formal mentoring programs have been created (a) to advise and support teachers in the early years of their careers (e.g., Little, 1990); (b) to support the development of students in traditionally disadvantaged groups (e.g., Tomlin, 1994); (c) to bring adult professionals to classrooms on a regular basis (e.g., EDC, 1994); or (d) to bring students into laboratories or other adult workplaces periodically (e.g., Waltner, 1992). Outcomes are as diverse as the programs themselves. Unfortunately, many worthwhile mentoring programs have not become widespread enough to have much influence on how students are educated in core subjects such as science. This is partly explained by the fact that they require unusual resources or entail large disruptions in the customary work routines of the volunteers.

TELEMENTORING

Because of these difficulties, the last several years have seen growing interest in the idea of using the Internet to support mentoring relationships. Existing telementoring programs take a variety of forms (Bennett, Hupert, Tsikalas & Meade, 1997; Harris & Jones, in press; Neils, 1997), yet all share the approach of orchestrating supportive relationships between adult volunteers and K-12 students that stretch over weeks or months. These on-line relationships often serve different purposes from traditional mentoring, and have unique needs for support and organization. Table 1 describes some of the differences between traditional mentoring, tutoring, apprenticeship, and curriculum-based telementoring as my collaborators and I have arranged it.

As suggested above, one of the main appeals of using Internet media such as e-mail or conferencing tools to develop and sustain mentoring relationships is to reduce the travel required for volunteers to maintain an active involvement in students' work. This allows adults outside the school to maintain lengthier and more intellectually involved relationships with students than would otherwise be possible. As Dan, a PhD student in Physics, said of his experience advising a group of three high school students studying black holes:

> I really enjoyed it, and for me it was great. I'd be sitting down, coding all day, writing [computer] programs, and I'd be able to take, you know, a half hour, an hour break every couple of days to answer this e-mail and look up something that I wanted to learn about.

The convenience of the time-delayed (or "asynchronous") communication that e-mail and other Internet media permit also has direct benefits for students, as one of my teacher collaborators explained to me in an interview:

> . . . For years in the educational environment we've been saying, oh yeah, we need . . . people coming in from businesses . . . but it's a very limited amount of time in your students' [lives]. For instance [a program I'm familiar with] sent lawyers into the classroom. And this is a very nice program, they'd be there every week for a period, over three weeks or four weeks. . . . But what if the kid, in the interim, thought of something, or had a dimension that they wanted to talk about? If the classroom teacher

wasn't in a position to discuss it with them, or didn't have the knowledge to discuss it with them, then it was on hold for a week. . . . [the Internet communication allows students to put their interests in an e-mail message] before it diminishes in their view of things that are crucial and important.

WHAT TELEMENTORING BRINGS TO THE CLASSROOM

The most compelling reason to orchestrate telementoring relationships for students is to take greater advantage of their unique personal interests. In many classrooms, the limits of a teacher's own time and expertise might make it necessary to confine their students' research to a narrow set of subjects. With the involvement of appropriate telementors, it becomes practical for students to pursue a variety of curriculum-related interests at the same time: one team researching earthquakes, another black holes, another the swimming motions of the plesiosaur. The added variety of students' work adds interest for both students and teachers.

As the next sections will illustrate, an important part of what a mentor does is facilitate students' best thinking by "problematizing" work which they might approach in a simplistic way. As most teachers

TABLE 1. Telementoring Contrasted with Other Helping Relationships

	Tutoring	Traditional Apprenticeship	Traditional Career Mentoring	Curriculum-Based Telementoring
Goal	Expertise in solving a well-defined set of problems (e.g., introductory computer programming, algebraic proofs)	Performance of a complex craft (e.g., sculpting, car repair, legal defense)	Performance in an organization or community of practice (e.g., an academic discipline or research community)	Understanding of a community of practice (e.g., environmental assessment)
Method/ purpose of problem selection	Tutor chooses and sequences problems to develop tutee's skills	Master chooses problems to maximize both apprentice's learning and the overall productivity of the shop	Mentee brings his/her problems to the mentor. Mentor hands down challenging and/or "plum" assignments with an eye to mentee's career development	Mentee brings his/her problems to the mentor. Mentor provides advice and challenging recommendations with an eye to mentee's best possible performance
Length of relationship	Possibly days, possibly years	Months or years	Usually months or years	Weeks or months

know who have tried to give students greater control over their own learning, inexperienced investigators often bite off more than they can chew, or trim a problem down to trivial proportions. Whitcomb once explained how the participation of mentors in students' work can motivate their efforts toward understanding:

> I'm hoping that by being involved with [their telementors], that they're putting [their work] out there for someone else, one, that they're going to be a little more critical of themselves, because it's not me that they've known for three years and they know that if they smile nicely I won't get so mad about it. . . . They'll have somebody new that they're presenting it to, and somebody who will give them a *different* kind of feedback than the feedback I've given them.

Telementors' role as a responsive and critical audience for students' work does seem to make a difference. In a study of one mature implementation of telementoring, I found that students who put forward greater effort to sustain their mentoring relationships over the course of their projects were significantly more likely to use sophisticated argument strategies in their final reports. In particular, they were more likely to anticipate possible objections to their work and weigh perspectives even-handedly (O'Neill, 1997; O'Neill, 1998). Most important, "good" students were not the only beneficiaries of this effect. Neither students' argument strategies nor their effort in sustaining their mentoring relationships were significantly correlated with their grades on a traditional content test.

Telementoring also provides some unique opportunities to increase students' awareness of adult careers. While telementoring relationships gain focus from students' school work, they can also provide opportunities for students to encounter adult work in a way that makes it more meaningful to them. One of my collaborators, Wagner, explained to me that his most important motivation in arranging telementoring relationships for his students was:

> . . . that the kids can see how scientists think, how they work. Not only get the information, because they're going to get that, because they could get that from anybody who's knowledgeable, but also the process of doing it.

Several examples of this type of guidance will appear in the examples below.

A SAMPLE TELEMENTORING RELATIONSHIP

Closer examination of one telementoring relationship may help clarify the benefits I have been describing. While neither the best nor the worst relationship I have studied, this example briefly illustrates some of the key facets of telementoring, and how they are influenced by events in the classroom. These issues will be re-visited in a later section when I discuss the design of telementored curriculum units.

One of my collaborators, Wagner, teaches Earth Science to mixed classes of 9th-to-12th grade students at a Chicago-area high school. Generally, these classes are populated by "science avoiders" seeking to satisfy a minimum requirement for graduation. Wagner's strategy to motivate them is to let them study deeply whatever most interests them within the scope of his course, from stars to the extinction of the dinosaurs. However, he imposes strict requirements on the methods and reporting of their research, and expects more thorough and original work than he would for shorter-term projects.

In the final quarter of the 1995/96 school year, a team of two students in Wagner's class decided to do a research project on earthquakes. Wagner matched this team with a Geology graduate student whom I will refer to as Mandy.[1] The following excerpts from Mandy's e-mail exchanges with the earthquakes team illustrate a few of the kinds of support and guidance, both intellectual and emotional, that a telementor can provide for students. (Note: A " > " at the beginning of a line indicates a quotation from the previous message in the exchange.)

The relationship began with a fairly typical "hello" message:

Date: Thu, 2 May 1996
Dear Mandy,
    We are juniors at New Trier High School. We are participating in a group project involving earthquakes. Your help would be greatly appreciated. Our project is due on May 17.
    Yours Truly,
    Marilyn and Robert

---

[1]A pseudonym. Throughout this article, only the two teachers are referred to by their real names. They have given their express consent to be identified.

Marilyn and Robert's initial greeting received a prompt and friendly reply. In it, Mandy attempts to help Marilyn and Robert set an agenda for their work. She cautions them about the shortness of their schedule, but tries to inspire confidence as well:

Date: Sat, 4 May 1996
Dear Marilyn and Robert,
Hello and welcome! Glad to hear from you. I'm really excited about working with you on this project.
> Our project is due on May 17.
Whew! Tight timeline, but I'm sure we can make it. My help is at your disposal. What aspect of earthquakes are you interested in? We first need to define the question/info that best grabs your interest, and then we can formulate a "research attack" plan for the project.
Draft a few ideas down on paper, then e-mail me back with the info. Once we have a good topic, we can hit the ground running.
If you're short on ideas, grab the local paper or the Tribune, or news magazines like Time, Newsweek, or even Discovery. With the recent earthquake in the Pacific Northwest, I'm sure the media has cooked up a few articles with cool graphics.

After this message, five days elapsed during which Robert and Marilyn brainstormed ideas for their project. This can be a very time-intensive process, because students must consider not only what they are curious about, but which of their curiosities can most likely be addressed to their teacher's satisfaction using available data. At the end of the five days, Robert broke the silence with Mandy by reporting the question that he and Marilyn had come up with:

Date: Thu, 9 May 1996
Dear Mandy,
I'm sorry about not really corresponding with you as much as I should . . . I'm starting to get nervous about not completing much on our project so far. The following is the exact question we are researching: Where and why do the largest earthquakes occur? Please write back. Thanx.
Your friend,
Robert

At this point in their exchange, Mandy sent Robert and Marilyn a long message suggesting a four-step process to completing their project. The steps, as she worded them, were:

1. Learn about earthquakes: what causes them and the three types of faults
2. What causes earthquakes: this is due to plate tectonics and you need to learn about the three plate boundary types: convergent, divergent, and strike slip . . . find out which one causes the deepest and strongest earthquakes
3. Where do the strongest EQ occur: find a world-wide map with dots showing the distribution of EQ the last decade or so. There are a few on the net but any intro Earth Science textbook should have such a map. Your local library has to have a text with it (school or city public library).
4. Match plate boundary location with the location of the strongest EQ: in doing this, you have defined the cause for the strongest EQ.

Robert was so impressed with this plan that in his next message, he expressed some concern about the amount of time that Mandy might be taking away from her job to help with his project. He also informed Mandy that the deadline for his final report had been extended. Note that in her response Mandy shares his relief, but stresses the importance of making good use of the additional time. She also requests a summary of the work he and Marilyn have done so that she can continue to offer informed advice:

Date: Tue, 14 May 1996
>It's me, Robert. I want you to know that I did get your rather
>large message sent on Friday. It will be very helpful.
>Thank you very much. Our new due-date is Monday, May 20,
>instead of Friday.
Alright! Deadline extensions are always a great feeling. Together we'll make sure to make the best of it!
As to the "four step plan," the approach is really that simple. And if you hit a stumbling block, just e-mail (or in last ditch effort as the deadline nears and you don't have computer access . . . call) because I have a small confession to make . . . I already know the answer to your thesis question. The steps I outlined last week are the exact same steps I put my undergraduates through to

answer the same question within a 50 minute lab. They have it easier since I provide all the necessary references; you have to find them on your own.

E-mail a quick research summary the next time you get on the computer; that way I know where you are and can drop suggestions to make sure your time isn't lost on unimportant sidetracks.

Another confession. . . . it doesn't take me that long to write these letters, so please don't worry about that. . . . It's . . . my "job" to help you though as much of the research snarls that I can for your project. I'm a teacher here at the university, and I make myself available to my students anytime during the day, except after Letterman has read the Top Ten :-)

If you want me to read your paper before you turn it in, just attach it to an e-mail message and I'll review it and e-mail back suggestions.

Talk to you tomorrow, Robert–Mandy

Three things are important to note about this message and the dialogue as a whole. First, this dialogue between Mandy and her mentees is driven by the project requirements and deadlines that the teacher has put in place. These both stimulate conversation and provide a common frame of reference in which the participants can work together to understand and accomplish challenging tasks. Second, Mandy's role is not simply that of an answer-provider; she helps Robert and Marilyn over "snarls" in their work, ensuring that they can exercise initiative and learn in a relatively independent way, without losing time on sidetracks.

Finally, the kind of personal attention which Mandy provides in this case does not guarantee that students' projects will be successful. The work is still up to them, and it is influenced by factors over which a telementor can have no control. Team partners miss school; they bicker; they fritter away time. The teacher is still responsible for mediating these factors and formally evaluating students' learning. However, with telementors sharing the burden of providing advice and guidance to students, they can often come closer to realizing the full potential of their ideas.

A TELEMENTORED UNIT IN MIDDLE SCHOOL SCIENCE: COMMUNITY IN BALANCE

Even if students are not yet prepared to conduct independent research, there are practical ways to make room for their varied curiosities in a more constrained curriculum unit. A good example is a unit titled "Community in Balance," designed by Whitcomb and I for the 1995/96 school year. This unit was implemented with a class composed of seventh and eight grade students at an inner-city school in Chicago. The 30 students involved represented a broad range of ability levels, including students described by school officials as behavior problems.

Community in Balance was launched six weeks from the end of the school year, and was largely intended to tie together themes and sub-ject-matter which the students had been working on all year. The starting point was a fictional scenario that each of them was to play a part in acting out. This scenario was presented in a brochure that read in part as follows:

> You are a member of a team of environmental engineers. Each team is comprised of people who have specialized in explorations of the following areas: soil, water, and health. A small community, Nadroj, has asked you to use your expertise as they determine whether or not a paper mill should be built in their community.
>
> Nadroj is a community that has experienced major economic problems in recent years. Once a steel mill provided a vast num-ber of jobs in the community. But in the past ten years, the mill had to cut back on employment and now it has closed down. . . .
>
> Recently, a proposal was made to construct a paper mill near the town. While the immediate reaction of the town council was to accept the proposal, there was strong opposition by govern-ment environmental agencies who feel that the paper mill will severely and negatively impact on the environmental health of the community. The debate in the city council has centered around the construction proposal. Each side has provided valid arguments for and against the construction of the paper mill. Tempers began to flare.
>
> In order to resolve the problem, you and the other environ-mental engineers have been asked by the community to examine the issues of possible soil and water damage and the related human health issues in order to provide a plan that will allow the construction to take place without major damage to the commu-nity's environment.

Whitcomb assigned her students to six teams of five students each, and gave each team a specialty to concentrate on in their environmental assessment: either air pollution, water pollution, or possible effects on human health. Each team was to prepare a position paper and deliver a briefing to the "city council" (the class) and the "mayor" (teacher), laying out the potential hazards they saw in building and operating the paper mill, as well as reasonable measures to manage them. The cost of various anti-pollution measures was to be taken into consideration so the community could choose a course of action which would balance its economic needs with its environmental health.

One of six volunteers was assigned to oversee each group's efforts to play the role of environmental consultant convincingly and offer credible recommendations to the town council. These volunteers included a city planner, two environmental engineers, and an employee of a state health department.

THE DESIGN OF COMMUNITY IN BALANCE

Table 2 provides a summary of the design for telementoring in the Community in Balance unit. Before describing how this unit was executed and what kinds of telementoring relationships it fostered, I will discuss each of its design elements and explain their importance to a telementored unit that will be worthwhile and repeatable from year to year.

Curricular Occasion

The most important design element in a telementored unit is the curriculum itself. While one might think that knowledgeable volunteers could add value to any curriculum related to their expertise, most curriculum is designed to make the classroom self-sufficient. In most

TABLE 2. Summary of Community in Balance Design for Telementoring

Curricular Occasion	Students play the role of environmental consultants, advising a town council on a construction proposal from a paper company.
Ratio of Students to Mentors	5:1
Length of Unit	5 weeks
Products Produced by Students	Position paper for "city council," oral presentation
Monitoring by Teacher	Thorough reading of email every 2 days

cases this leaves telementors with very little to do; and students, for their part, cannot be expected to put forward the effort to be good mentees if they cannot see how maintaining a relationship with a mentor will help them to work and learn better. For these reasons and others, the units which make the best candidates for telementoring are ones in which teachers feel they have not been able to do justice to the curiosities of their students–either because the teacher's knowledge is too thin, or because it seemed impossible to manage so many disparate threads of inquiry at once.

Ratio of Students to Mentors

Teachers know how much better they can teach a smaller class. Similarly, the unique quality of interaction between adults and students in a telementoring relationship has much to do with the ratio of students to mentors. In the example I gave above, Mandy could share her expert advice with Robert and Marilyn in a few spare minutes each day. Apply the spare minutes of 6 or 8 mentors to a single science class, and types of constructivist teaching become practical which may not have been before.

I estimate that the number of university-educated adults in the U.S. and Canada who might volunteer for telementoring could be as high as 2.9 million (O'Neill, 1998). While this is not enough to provide one-to-one telementoring for all students, relationships like Mandy, Marilyn and Robert's could be within reach of most students if each mentor worked with small groups of students for a few weeks each year, and worked with more than one group per year. Elsewhere I have discussed the design of information systems that will help telementors locate and enter into new mentor relationships quickly (O'Neill & Gomez, 1998).

Activity Structure

After the curriculum and the student-to-mentor ratio, the most important design element to consider for telementored units is the set of roles and responsibilities for the participants, including students, telementors, *and* the teacher. In the past, I have asked teachers to describe these roles in an "activity structure" that shows the stages of the unit and spells out what each of the participants should be contributing during each stage. It is best if each stage has an associated "milestone" assignment so that students and their mentors have clear tasks around which to converse.

Students and their mentors should be able to see clearly how each milestone contributes to the final goals of the unit, and use them to monitor their own progress. A sample activity structure for the Balanced Community project is provided in Appendix A.

Length of Unit

Because the work schedules and routines of schools and adult workplaces differ so greatly, it is important for telementored units to include some buffer time to accommodate slips in schedule. Although e-mail travels quickly, there will often be a lag of a day or two before a mentor can respond to students' work. If mentors' paid work takes them away from the office, these delays can stretch to several days. Likewise in the school environment, assemblies and school holidays can cause delays that volunteer mentors don't anticipate. As Table 2 shows, we budgeted 5 weeks for Community in Balance. In retrospect, the 7 or 8 weeks that Wagner normally budgets would have allowed for greater closure.

Monitoring by the Teacher

Most of the teachers and researchers with whom I have discussed telementoring feel it is necessary to monitor communications between their mentors and students on a regular basis; either to assuage parents' concerns about adult volunteers in an atmosphere of media hype about "net sex," to protect mentors from unreasonable requests by students, or to protect students from overly-demanding mentors. While friction between students and their mentors is very rare, this does not make monitoring unnecessary.

In the Community in Balance unit, Whitcomb reviewed every e-mail message her students exchanged with her 6 volunteers. Because she had decided to involve only her home room class in the unit, the quantity of e-mail was not too overwhelming to read every other day; and while she rarely needed to intervene in students' relationships with their mentors, she found the monitoring itself had an unexpected benefit. Monitoring her students' conversations with their mentors allowed her to "step back" from her position as a teacher and observe ways in which her directions had been misunderstood:

> I have gotten a lot of good information [from the email] as far as where there's breakdowns when I ask the kids to do something

. . . or something that isn't clear. . . . That was very helpful for me, and gave me a lot of insights that I'm going to try to specifically address when I set up a project like this again.

TELEMENTORING DIALOGUES
IN COMMUNITY IN BALANCE

In an earlier section, I showed the path a single telementoring relationship took in one of Wagner's classes. Next, I will profile the relationships that took place across Whitcomb's entire class during the Community in Balance unit. Along the way, I will mention the relative frequencies with which students and their mentors discussed particular topics or aspects of their work. These data were compiled using a coding scheme developed with a software program for qualitative research called QSR NUD*IST (QSR, 1997). This coding scheme, which was applied on a line-by-line basis to every e-mail message, includes some 50 non-exclusive categories representing the topics of conversation and conversational "moves" I observed in a larger dataset of 26 telementoring relationships. Because the objective of the coding was to support interpretive analysis such as case studies, rather than statistical measures, no reliability coding was done.

Getting to Know You

Whitcomb was concerned with establishing trust between her students and their mentors early on, so she began the Balanced Community project by handing each research team a short, one-page autobiography by its assigned telementor. She and I requested these from our volunteers soon after they agreed to participate in the unit. After students read their mentors' biographies, they responded with ones of their own describing their ages, likes and dislikes, and their favorite subjects in school. An example shows how friendly students' biographies often were:

Date: Wed, 15 May 1996 18:54:45-0500
To: mentor@covis.nwu.edu
From: brandi@schools.covis.nwu.edu
Subject: All about me
Hello! My name is Brandi Thomas. I'm 12 years old and in the seventh grade. I like to dance and sing, and hope to be a singer

when I grow up. I like to read Goosebumps books, I have 14 books. I have 3 sisters and 3 brothers, I'm the second youngest out of seven kids. I use to live on the west side but now I live on the north side. I stay with my aunt and she takes care of me.

I have a cousin, she's in 8th grade, she's about to graduate from grammar school and I have a dog her name is Spotty.

P.S. Im looking foward to you respond.

Our six volunteers took quite different approaches in responding to their mentees' biographies. Two of them chose not to respond to them at all, taking them merely as background; but the most popular telementors responded to each biography individually, sometimes in an almost childlike fashion:

Date: 16 May 1996 08:38:08 PST
From: paul@local.agency.gov
Subject: All about me
To: mentor@covis.nwu.edu
Subject: All about me
Hey Brandi! It's great to meet you. I also have a 12 year old daughter named Noelle. She also likes Goosebumps books and all sorts of scary stuff. And I like to sing too! When I'm not working at my job I play guitar and sing in a rock & roll band. My dog's name is Midnight. She's mostly black and very furry. I'm really looking forward to working with you and your team.
Paul
Principal Planner/Environmental Coordinator
Sunnyplace, CA

Whitcomb felt that the personal gestures made by mentors like Paul made her students more responsive to advice later on. In our closing interview, she brought up the case of Trevor and Craig, two normally disengaged teammates who were impressed with their mentor's curiosity over Trevor's favorite pastime, gymnastics. Trevor had referred to this in his biography as "flipping," and his mentor Parker, not being familiar with this term, had asked what it meant. Whitcomb explained the significance of Parker's question to Trevor and Craig:

For my level [of students], I think [the telementors' personal responses to the biographies were] very important. Now, Craig is very motivated, just very scattered. Trevor is not motivated at all. But they both at the end made a big effort to put this project together, and to write back to [Parker]. And I think that the key to it was the fact that they felt he really cared about them. Because he asked about flipping. Just a little tiny thing; and then to write back and say, "Oh! That's cool. Now I know what that is." I think that personal thing is important for this to work well with the junior high.

Some are surprised to find that curriculum-based mentoring relationships are not usually deeper than this. Students and mentors will occasionally grow closer, but one should not be disappointed if this does not happen. Whitcomb put the proper perspective on the issue of friendship in mentoring in one of our interviews:

> . . . a friend is someone we bum around with, have fun with, and everything else. Although I think there has to be a certain bond of friendship if a mentoring situation is going to be positive . . . when I say "friendship" I mean "comfort zone": Trusting you enough to know that if I do screw up really badly, or ask a really dumb question, you will be tolerant enough to help me see where my mistake was. . . .

Domain-Centered Dialogue

After the introductions had been made, the bulk of students' correspondence with their telementors in the Balanced Community unit centered on the phenomena and issues they needed to understand to draft their proposals for the paper mill. These issues were far removed from the daily life of students in an inner-city school in Chicago. For instance, how is paper typically made? What materials are used? What pollutants can be generated in this process (including chemicals, thermal pollution, and so on)? How might these emissions harm plants, animals, and people, and what strategies and technology are available to reduce the impact of these pollutants?

On the whole, Whitcomb's volunteers devoted the largest volume of text in their messages to explanations of the phenomena or the practices of environmental assessment. However, the relationships were not entirely cerebral. Mentors used just slightly less space offering encouragement to their mentees, and making suggestions about how they should get their work done (Table 3). And despite the expectation that some

TABLE 3. Percentage of Mentor Message Text Devoted to Various Conversational Moves

	Explanations	Encouragement	Suggestions/ Advice	Questions
Percentage of total mentor message text	38	30	21	11

students had of their mentors serving as answer mills, our volunteers asked many questions of their own. In fact, they spent nearly a third as much text posing their own questions for students as they did providing explanations of the phenomena that students were studying.

The separate categories listed in Table 3 might give the wrong impression of how intertwined various forms of guidance and support can be in telementoring. The excerpt below from one e-mail exchange shows how mentors sometimes artfully combined explanations of domain phenomena with heuristic questions:

> Let's think about what happens inside of a paper mill. Paper is made from wood and sometimes from recycled paper. . . . These materials are ground up and mixed with water to make a sort of paste that is then squished into sheets of paper. But along the way, lots of chemicals are added to this "paste." These chemicals are used to make the paper whiter, stronger, shinier and so on. Many of these chemicals are hazardous or poisonous to animals and plants. . . . When the paste is squished into paper, most of the water comes out and many of these chemicals are contained in the water. This water now becomes waste from the paper mill and has to go somewhere, right? Some paper mills dig large ponds in the ground where they discharge this water. Now, go and read the note I sent to you on Friday. How do you think all of this would affect the soil where the pond is?

In both the message above and the one below, specific actions are suggested for students to take, but opportunities are left open for them to take initiative. The following mentor's unpretentious introduction to soil science, and his reassurances about difficult-looking vocabulary are good examples of how mentors can help students to approach tasks which they might otherwise find intimidating:

I don't have many books for kids but you might be able to get some information and ideas out of Paul Ehrlich and Anne Ehrlich, Population, Resources, and Environment: W.H.Freeman and Co. Look in the index under soil and you will see several pages of stuff about soils. . . . There will be a lot in a book like this that you won't understand, but you may be surprised at how much you can understand. Don't worry about all of the ridiculous names they give to different soils like entisols and vertisols. You don't need to know them. . . . But you can get the idea that soils are about half minerals and the other half is dead organic material and lots of bugs, worms, bacteria, fungi, and air and water.

Status Reports

Status reports from students are a vitally important source of fodder for a mentor's advice and guidance (O'Neill & Gomez, 1998, November). As I often explain to students, a mentor is like a wilderness guide: if she doesn't know where you are and where you want to go, she can't provide you with good advice on how to get there. Whitcomb's activity structure design for Community in Balance (Appendix A) required her students to submit a number of "milestone" assignments both to her and their mentors. These included an initial set of research questions and a later statement of research focus. An example is given below:

To: mentor@covis.nwu.edu
From: dmadison@schools.covis.nwu.edu (Dara Madison)
Subject: our group's focus
Dear Mr. More

Our teacher has made us choose a main problem we want to focus on from our questions and this is what we are focusing on. We are focusing on is what the cutting down of the forest will do to the soil like what kind of erosion it may cause that might make a slope and hit the town or might deposit all the nutrients of the soil into a nearby body of water which in turn make the soil poor so that the people will not be able to farm on it or no trees will grow. Now were not asking you to give us any answers but we haven't been able to find a lot of information on these subjects and were wondering if you knew any web sites on the net or any books we could check out about these things.

P.S. We would be thankful for any help you could give us
Our group,
Soil 1

Perhaps because of the level of trust established through the formal biographical exchanges (which took up approximately 50% of the students' message text), students offered little resistance to sharing these milestones with their mentors. They also maintained a healthful balance between asking questions and reporting on the status of their work: each made up approximately 12% of the total text in their exchanges with mentors (see Table 4).

Discussing Mentors' Work

Considering the bridge metaphor offered at the opening of this paper, one of the most satisfying aspects of the Community in Balance project was the natural opportunity it provided for mentors to explain various aspects of professional practice in Environmental Science to students. For example, one student mentioned her dislike of "snobs" in her biography. Her mentor, who worked for the Environmental Protection Agency and was a former environmental planner, responded with an explanation of "snob zoning":

> Incidentally, one of the important elements of a project like the proposed paper mill is the effect of "snob zoning" which means that some people don't want to put up with other people's proposals because they want to protect their "investment" in a neighborhood, or a community. So they "zone" out the possibilities of having undesirable industry or in some cases, economic development, in order to prevent it from happening. Sometimes this is done by requiring large fees for permits, sometimes it is managed by requiring large expenses for property lots. . . . So when you are looking at the plusses and minuses of this project, don't object and find ways to prevent the project from happening based on "snobbishness"!

Exchanges like this one are uniquely valuable because they are natural outgrowths of a productive conversation, rather than isolated career day events.

DESIGN GUIDELINES FOR TELEMENTORING

While there are no cookie-cutter solutions to designing telementored units, the experiences reported here suggest some general guidelines for readers who may wish to run their own telementored units.

TABLE 4. Percentage of Student Message Text Devoted to Various Conversational Moves

	Biography	Project Ideas	Questions	Status Reports
Percentage of total student message text	50	20	12	12

Clarify the Expectations, and Communicate them Early

Before volunteers are recruited, it is important to clarify what their duties will be. Detailed case studies of both successful and failed telementoring relationships (O'Neill, 1998) have shown that volunteers are often quite concerned about "giving answers away." In the course of any ambitious project, students will encounter "snags" that slow them down and offer little opportunity for learning. However, there may also be challenges from which a great deal could be learned. What distinguishes snags from learning opportunities depends entirely on the teaching goals set out for the unit, so it is important that these be clear. When students make what they believe are reasonable requests of their mentors and are rebuffed with the assertion that "I know the answer to your question, but I don't think I should tell you," they feel teased, and may suspect their mentors of mean-spiritedness or egotism. The only way to avoid this "teasing dynamic" between mentors and students is to be sure that they are aware of the expectations at the beginning of the project. After teaching objectives are laid out for the unit, they should be communicated with both mentors and students as early as possible.

Recruiting Volunteers

Locating the right volunteers for any particular curriculum piece can be a challenge. Friends or relatives with expertise that will be useful often make the best starting place. Studies of volunteer activity (Duchesne, 1989; Hall et al., 1998; Hayghe, 1991) have shown that most volunteers have little in common besides being asked to volunteer by someone they know. Companies, government agencies and universities in the local community are also good targets, though I have found that small organizations are usually more cooperative than large ones.

My own interviews with past telementors suggest that the kinds of people most likely to make reliable volunteers are those who enjoy working with children and find the idea of telementoring itself intriguing. Here are a few key points to remember in recruiting efforts:

- Begin recruiting a month or more before the unit starts. Sometimes finding the people needed takes more than one attempt.
- Asking a lot of people for a little of their time is generally a more successful strategy than asking just a few people for a lot of their time.
- Tell potential volunteers before the beginning of the project how many minutes per week are expected from them, and how many times per week they are expected to respond to their mentees.
- Take time to write a careful, two-or-three paragraph description of the school and the class(es) that will be involved in the telementored unit. Volunteers will appreciate this, because much of their satisfaction comes from knowing who they are helping and why they need help.
- After the potential volunteers have been made aware of the expectations, give them a chance to back out. Volunteers who give their time grudgingly are usually of little help.

Retaining Volunteers

It is important to understand the kinds of activities that most gratify mentors if telementoring is to be an ongoing part of students' experience in school. If the units are run well, recruiting gets easier from year to year, because satisfied volunteers return. While most volunteers don't mind serving as guides to learning resources such as web pages, books and magazines, they usually want to do something more than act as librarians. Part of the thrill of research is figuring out what questions to ask, so most mentors want to help students shape questions. Nearly all mentors also want see the final results of their mentees' work, so they can see how students applied their advice and whether it was useful. As one volunteer, who did not get a copy of his mentees' final report, explained, "It's kind of like if you're tutoring math–you want to know how the kid did on the exam afterward."

Maintaining Visibility

When telementoring relationships fail, it is usually because the progress of student's work has not been made visible enough to mentors for them to offer informed advice. One frustrated mentor who was interviewed described her attempts to offer guidance to a group of non-communicative students as "working in a black box." Having students complete milestone assignments and share them with their mentors is helpful in preventing total silence; but ultimately, healthy mentoring relationships are based on a sense of mutual responsibility. For students, the starting-place is a faith that even if their mentors are not world experts, they can offer useful advice when given a chance.

The Teacher's Role

While telementors can bring a great deal to the classroom, there remain important tasks they cannot do, either because they do not have a teacher's training and experience, or because much of the support that students need cannot be provided remotely. It is useful to think of telementoring as a kind of team teaching arrangement. While some students are busy corresponding with telementors and following up on their suggestions, the teacher can be helping other students to conduct Internet searches, graph and interpret data, or revise their written reports. However, the division of labor involved here is not such that one can draw up a list of teaching tasks for the unit, draw a line through the middle, and hand off half to the mentors. From time to time, mentors will not be able to meet students' needs in as timely a way as is needed. In these cases, a teacher must be prepared to step in and make up the difference.

Another indispensable role that teachers play in telementoring is in helping students to interpret their mentors' advice. While most of the mentors involved in this work have real talent in "writing to the students' level," students will still sometimes have difficulty seeing the value of the advice their mentors offer. The telementors have only written cues to tell them whether students have understood and profited from their advice. They cannot see the confusion in the students' faces if their instructions or explanations are unclear. Teachers, however, can. If they overhear complaints such as "he's no help," teachers must be ready to serve as interpreters of mentors' advice.

FUTURE DIRECTIONS

As I hope this article has shown, telementoring is a complex innovation with much potential and many avenues for improvement. In my current research, I am exploring several of these. First, in collaboration with the CSILE/Knowledge-Building team at OISE/UT, I am investigating the potential of educational groupware systems to permit more flexible and more sustainable arrangements for telementoring. I am also developing a new web-based application to lighten the organizational burden that telementoring places on teachers, and enable corporations and other adult workplaces to more easily undertake telementoring as a form of educational outreach and staff development.

Finally, under a new grant, the Knowledge-Building team and I will be exploring in depth the benefits that adult volunteers derive from telementoring, and developing a set of empirically-based guidance materials for them and the organizations in which they work. In the longer term, I hope to design larger curriculum-based interventions in which telementoring will play an enabling role. I am currently considering a program related to black history in North America.

REFERENCES

Bennett, D. T., Hupert, N., Tsikalas, K., & Meade, T. (1997). *Telementoring: Designing on-line mentoring environments for high school women in science and technical courses.* Paper presented at the Joint National Conference of the Women in Engineering Program Advocates and the National Association of Minority Engineering Program Administrators, Washington, DC.

Chapman, G. (1998, June 15). Digital nation: Push to trade class textbooks for laptop PCs is a misuse of technology. Los Angeles Times, pp. D4.

Duchesne, D. (1989). *Giving freely: Volunteers in Canada* (Labor Analytic Report 4). Ottawa, Canada: Statistics Canada.

EDC. (1994). *Industry volunteers in the classroom: Freeing teachers' time for professional development* : Educational Development Center, Inc., Newtonville, MA

Hall, M., Knighton, T., Reed, P., Bussiere, P., McRae, D., & Bowen, P. (1998). *Caring Canadians, involved Canadians: Highlights from the 1997 national survey of giving, volunteering and participating* (71-542-X1E): Statistics Canada.

Harris, J. B., & Jones, G. (in press). A descriptive study of telementoring among students, subject matter experts, and teachers: Message flow and function patterns. *Journal of research on computing in education.*

Hayghe, H. V. (1991, February). Volunteers in the U.S.: Who donates the time? *Monthly Labor Review,* 17-23.

Jacobi, M. (1991). Mentoring and undergraduate academic success: A literature review. *Review of Educational Research, 61,* 505-532.

Kram, K. E. (1985). *Mentoring at work: Developmental relationships in organizational life.* New York: University Press of America.

Lave, J., & Wenger, E. (1991). *Situated learning: Legitimate peripheral participation.* New York. Cambridge University Press.

Little, J. W. (1990). The mentor phenomenon and the social organization of teaching. *Review of Research in Education, 16,* 297-351.

Neils, D. (1997). The Hewlett-Packard e-mail mentor program. Available: http://mentor.external.hp.com/.

O'Neill, D. K. (1997, March). *Bluffing their way into science: Analyzing students' appropriation of the Research Article genre.* Paper presented at the American Educational Research Association, Chicago, IL.

O'Neill, D. K. (1998). *Engaging science practice through science practitioners: Design experiments in K-12 telementoring.* Unpublished doctoral dissertation, Northwestern University.

O'Neill, D. K., & Gomez, L. M. (1994). *The Collaboratory Notebook: A networked knowledge-building environment for project learning.* Paper presented at the Ed-Media '94: World Conference on Educational Multimedia and Hypermedia, Vancouver, BC, Canada.

O'Neill, D. K., & Gomez, L. M. (1998, November). *Sustaining mentoring relationships on-line.* Paper presented at the ACM Conference on Computer-Supported Cooperative Work, Seattle, WA.

O'Neill, D. K., Wagner, R., & Gomez, L. M. (1996). Online mentors: Experimenting in science class. *Educational Leadership, 54*(3), 39-42.

Phillips-Jones, L. (1982). *Mentors and proteges.* New York: Arbor House.

QSR. (1997). NUD*IST (Version 4.0). Thousand Oaks, CA: Scolari.

Robertson, H. J. (1998). *No more teachers, no more books: The commercialization of Canada's schools.* Toronto: McClelland & Stewart, Inc.

Scardamalia, M., & Bereiter, C. (1996). Engaging students in a knowledge society. *Educational Leadership, 54*(3), 6-10.

Scardamalia, M., & Bereiter, C. (1997). Adaptation and Understanding: A case for new cultures of schooling. In S. Vosniadou, E. D. Corte, R. Glaser, & H. Mandl (Eds.), *International perspectives on the psychological foundations of technology-based learning environments.*

Soloway, E., & Norris, C. (1998). Using technology to address old problems in new ways. *Communications of the ACM, 41*(8), 11-18.

Tomlin, V. E. (1994). *A mentor program for improving the academic attainment of black adolescent males.* Unpublished doctoral dissertation, University of Denver, Denver, CO.

Vygotsky, L. S. (1978). *Mind in Society.* Cambridge, MA: Harvard University.

Waltner, J. C. (1992). Learning from scientists at work. *Educational Leadership, 49*(6), 48-52.

Wighton, D. J. (1993). *Telementoring: An examination of the potential for an educational network*: Education Technology Centre of British Columbia.

Appendix A. Sample Activity Structure

Stage of Project Cycle	Students	Mentor	Teacher
Introduction	Introduce themselves to their mentors	Introduce him/herself to the mentees	– explain the role of the mentor in the project – distribute guidelines for telementoring – explain the role of the students as they interact with the mentor
Set the Scenario	– Describe the project to the mentor – Describe the task of their group in the project	Ask students any questions necessary to clarify the nature and purpose of the project and help them focus on the problem	– aid the student in answering the mentor's questions, if they are having difficulty with interpretation or explanation – review communication to make sure that the students are on the right track
Project Proposal	Explain the "plan of attack": – how they will go about investigating the problem – how the information will be presented to the town council (peers) and mayor (teacher)	– review the plan for investigation and presentation – point out logical procedure for investigation – comment on the elements for the presentation that are professionally acceptable	– review mentors' comments. – bridge the comments with realistic expectations in respect to students' development and experience – discuss with the students those suggestions which are feasible and "doable"
Drafts of Milestones	Provide the mentor with all the drafts or milestones submitted to the teacher	provide critical commentary and positive reinforcement to students and teacher	review mentor's feedback with each group
Between Milestones	Request help in locating resources, collecting and/or interpreting data, reformulating questions, etc.	Make all reasonable efforts in helping students to understand data and other resources, point them to other sources, clarify their questions, analyze results and draw conclusions	
Final Product	Provide mentor with final paper	Make recommendations to the teacher with respect to students' evaluation, including but not limited to: effort, quality, logical progression from problem to final product	Consider mentor's recommendation, consult with students if necessary, determine grade as seems fit

Creating Computer-Mediated Communities of Practice in Special Education

Ken Ryba

Massey University Albany

Linda Selby

Auckland College of Education

Louis J. Kruger

Northeastern University

SUMMARY. The convergence of theory and research on socially shared cognition represents a promising new direction for understanding how to enhance the intellectual growth of individuals. In this article, we draw upon the metaphor of "apprenticeship" to explain how individual cognitive development of children and adults alike can be enhanced by mentoring relationships within a particular educational "culture." The view advanced here is that computers and related technologies can be instrumental in creating socially interactive and reflective learning communities. Within these communities there is active transmission of knowledge between individuals as they are guided from the periphery through to the center of the learning enterprise. Examples of communities of learners are provided to illustrate the process of socially shared cognition and development of knowledge networks. Principles for the creation of sustainable learning communities apply equally to traditional educational settings and on-line com-

Address correspondence to: Ken Ryba, Coordinator, Educational Psychology Training Programme, Massey University Albany, Private Bag 102 904, North Shore MSC, New Zealand.

[Haworth co-indexing entry note]: "Creating Computer-Mediated Communities of Practice in Special Education." Ryba, Ken, Linda Selby, and Louis J. Kruger. Co-published simultaneously in *Special Services in the Schools* (The Haworth Press, Inc.) Vol. 17, No. 1/2, 2001, pp. 59-76; and: *Computers in the Delivery of Special Education and Related Services: Developing Collaborative and Individualized Learning Environments* (ed: Louis J. Kruger) The Haworth Press, Inc., 2001, pp. 59-76. Single or multiple copies of this article are available for a fee from The Haworth Document Delivery Service [1-800-342-9678, 9:00 a.m. - 5:00 p.m. (EST). E-mail address: getinfo@haworthpressinc.com].

59

munities. The concept of the "collective zone of proximal development" is advanced here to explain how cognitive growth progressively occurs for community members who are operating within a socially interactive and reflective learning environment. Finally, principles and recommendations are offered on how to design communities so that all individuals can achieve their optimal functioning level through guided social participation. *[Article copies available for a fee from The Haworth Document Delivery Service: 1-800-342-9678. E-mail address: <getinfo@haworth pressinc.com> Website: <http://www.HaworthPress.com>]*

KEYWORDS. Internet, communities, apprenticeship, computers

INTRODUCTION

The presence of computers in education has given rise to some dramatic rethinking about the teaching and learning process. Early ideas of computer assisted instruction have given way to thinking about the social construction of knowledge in which individuals learn through interaction with one another rather than being "taught" by the computer. An exciting feature of this shift in thinking is the recognition that computers and other forms of information technology offer a context for not only enhancing individual performance but for creating communities of highly capable learners. This is evident in the widespread use of computers in educational settings as a basis for collaborative learning and enterprising new projects at all educational levels (Ryba, 1996). The more recent availability of the Internet for teachers to use to support school curriculum activities as well as for their own professional development purposes, has provided the context for the establishment of on-line communities of practice. The Internet consists of intersecting communities of people who communicate using computer networks. These networks enable teachers, special service providers, and students to meet and communicate with people and learn together. Contemporary thinking about "communities of practice" represent a dynamic new way of understanding how to develop human potential.

THE SOCIAL CONTEXT OF COGNITIVE GROWTH WITH COMPUTERS

Contrary to early concerns about the dehumanizing effects of learning with technology, computers have provided a context for bringing students together. There is vast evidence of the benefits to be derived from interactive teaching methods such as cooperative learning in which students and teachers work side by side (Ryba & Anderson, 1990; Frazer, Moltzen & Ryba, 1995). Increasingly, recognition has been given to the fact that collaboration and ability to relate to others is a vital aspect of effectiveness as a learner. A major effect of information technology is that it has caused us to think again about how people learn and what they are capable of achieving. This was evident in a project the first author carried out with trainees in a sheltered workshop who learned a simple version of the LOGO computer language. The trainees became so proficient at using LOGO graphics that they were asked to teach students at a nearby school how to do it. This was successful and as a result, LOGO became very popular at that school (Ryba & Anderson, 1990).

The interesting point about this early project was that the young adult trainees with intellectual disabilities were more than capable tutors. Not only did they teach school students but they also demonstrated how to use new software to university students enrolled in a computer education course. Before becoming computer tutors these trainees were performing mundane repetitive jobs such as packing dog biscuits and rolling newspapers into fire logs. The computer provided a situation in which we could see their capabilities and celebrate their learning achievements. It is important not to underestimate students' abilities. What we discovered from using computers is that students of all ability levels are capable learners and that technology is educationally and personally transforming when it is used to create better conditions for learning.

The effectiveness of the computer environment for all students depends upon the ability of the teacher to facilitate the teaching and learning process. Seymour Papert (1980) in his well known book *Mindstorms: Children, Computers and Powerful Ideas* was one of the first to point out that computers had the potential to transform the way students learn. Papert also had some important things to say about the role of the teacher as an anthropologist whose job it was to study how to facilitate students' learning by providing them with the resources they needed to build their intellectual structures. By studying the surrounding culture, teachers could guide students' participation in the learning process and enable them to make effective use of the intellectual tools through networking with other people.

SITUATED LEARNING IN COMMUNITIES OF PRACTICE

Lave (1988) argued that learning takes place as a function of the activity, context and culture in which it occurs. Learning is thus "situated" within a definite social and cultural context, and domain of learning. This contrasts with most classroom-based learning activities in which knowledge is abstract and presented out of context. According to Lave, social interaction is a critical component of situated learning. Learners become involved in a "community of practice" which embodies certain beliefs and behaviors to be acquired. At the outset, learners begin their journey at the periphery of this community and progress toward the center as they become more active and engaged within the culture. They move from being a newcomer or novice toward assuming the role of expert or old-timer. Moreover, situated learning is usually not directly taught but is unintentional, occurring through active participation in working together with other people. These ideas are what Lave and Wenger (1991) referred to as the process of "legitimate peripheral participation." Such participation is socially interactive in nature, involving an apprenticeship and guided participation between "newcomers" and "old-timers" within the educational community.

THE CONCEPT OF "APPRENTICESHIP" AND "GUIDED PARTICIPATION"

Anthropological studies of apprenticeship offer alternative ways of understanding the social processes of learning. Lave (1988) drew upon experiences in other cultures, such as craft apprenticeship in West Africa and apprenticeship among Yucatec Mayan midwives, to illustrate there are highly valued forms of knowledgeable skill in these cultures for which learning is structured in apprentice-like forms. The perspective of "guided participation" in communities of practice is highly relevant also to many others forms of socially organized activity that have become accepted within Western society as sites of learning. For example, sports and leisure communities guide their newcomers through a scaffolded sequence of learning steps so that they progress from the periphery to the center of the activity. Likewise, service and community organizations convey a set of values and beliefs which guide their practices and influence induction of the novice into the expert membership of the organization (e.g., Alcoholics Anonymous, community service clubs).

In contrast to the above, many institutional educational arrangements are problematic in that they restrict the formation of communities of practice through requiring that skills be taught in isolation and out of context. The effect of this is that students have no sense of being within a community and that there is no process for making progress in learning through socially shared cognitions. According to Lave (1988), the main concern centers around the competitive nature of many learning environments in which learning is treated as an individualistic activity rather than a shared enterprise. From this perspective, learning within contemporary life has taken place within relatively alienated conditions. The effect of this is to diminish the identity of oneself to that of an isolated individual rather than as a member of a community of practice who is aspiring to gain mastery of knowledgeable skills.

Although there are obvious differences between apprenticeships involving mature learners and guided participation involving children, there are some common principles of interactive learning that apply to all students. Justification for the value of an interactive apprenticeship model has been provided by Rogoff (1990) who makes the following points:

1. Apprentices are active in gathering information and practicing skills as they participate in skilled activities. Children are active in observing and participating in the activities of those around them and they are motivated to participate more centrally.

2. The learning of apprentices is structured by practices developed by their predecessors to meet societally valued goals. This aspect of apprenticeship provides a parallel with the importance of recognizing that children's cognitive development involves learning to use the intellectual tools of their society (literacy, mnemonic devices, conventions for representing space) to implement culturally valued activities and goals.

3. Apprentices are assisted in their learning by communication and involvement with more skilled people (i.e., experts) and more advanced apprentices, who help determine how to divide the activity into sub-goals that the novice can begin to attain, as well as to provide pointers on how to handle the tools and skills required.

4. Apprentices seldom learn alone. In addition to being involved with more skilled practitioners, apprentices often learn in a com-

munity of fellow novices (such as fellow graduate students, classmates, siblings). Interaction with and observation of other novices provides challenge, support, collaborative solving of problems, and models of learning in progress.

Vygotsky (1978, 1987) argued that children's interactions with others in the "zone of proximal development" provide children with the opportunity to carry out cognitive processes jointly that are more advanced than they could manage independently, and that this joint problem-solving process can serve as the basis for children's subsequent independent efforts. Our concept of the "Collective" Zone of Proximal Development is an attempt to extend and combine Rogoff's ideas about guided participation with Vygotsky's notion of the zone of proximal development.

THE "COLLECTIVE" ZONE
OF PROXIMAL DEVELOPMENT

Vygotsky (1978, 1987) theorized that individual cognitive development is embedded in a sociocultural environment that provides tools for thinking and formation of partnerships. According to Vygotsky, student's interactions with others in the "zone of proximal development" (ZPD) enable students to carry out cognitive processes jointly that are more advanced than would be possible independently, and that these shared problem solving processes serve as a basis for subsequent independent efforts. Extending the concept of the ZPD, the view advanced here is that a group of students can form an "intellectual collective" in which there is the potential for all members to advance their learning through guidance from more capable peers. Both participation and guidance are mutual efforts of students and their companions which can result in advances in learning for all participants.

Figure 1 displays a model for understanding the operation of the collective zone of proximal development. It illustrates a movement from the current zone of functioning for a group of individuals through a collective zone in which scaffolded learning is provided through guidance and participation in the community. Within the community, individuals gain a sense of self-efficacy through reflective practice which motivates them to achieve. This sense of self-efficacy is enhanced as individuals experience success that is recognized and rewarded by others. The knowledge and skills gained through making

FIGURE 1. Ecological Analysis of the Collective Zone of Proximal Development

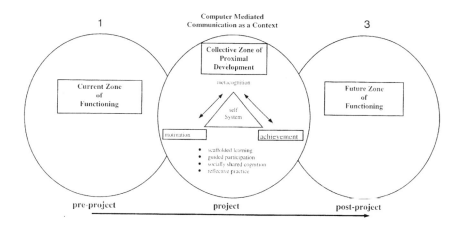

contributions to the community leads not only to positive perceptions of ability but to the formation of an identity as an effective and contributing member of the community. It is through guided participation that individuals progress from the periphery to the center of the learning environment.

COMMUNITIES OF PRACTICE AND LEARNING IN ACTION

The communities of practice framework stresses that developing a sense of identity as a community member, as well as becoming knowledgeable and skillful are all part of the same process. Self identity is crucial for motivating, shaping, and giving meaning to the development of skills (Rogoff, 1990). As students are guided in their participation to become increasingly self sufficient, they gain a sense of identity and a sense of effectiveness as learners. This personal development process is illustrated through the following computer mediated projects.

Learning with Multimedia at Patricia Avenue School (Hamilton, New Zealand)

Multimedia projects provide an ideal context for building a community of practice in the classroom in which students participate alongside the teacher in a cognitive apprenticeship model. Educators can relate multimedia applications to almost every area of the curriculum, and students with diverse abilities can use them. At Patricia Avenue School this included students with severe multiple disabilities. Working with computers and creating multimedia projects provided an opportunity for students to exercise personal control over both the technology and the learning process. Through controlling the computer they were able to become active participants and explore and develop an understanding of cause-and-effect relationships.

The students started with an easy-to-use multimedia software program for creating their own interactive materials. At first they used existing files that came with the program. One of their favorites was "Old McDonald's Farm" because they were able to use the existing sounds and graphics as well as create some of their own. When a student clicked on the animal it made a sound. In the next step, students used a computer program called "Our House." Students were able to click on different parts of the house and see what was in each room. In the process of building the house and contents, students were involved in gathering information and practicing skills as they participated in the activities.

The classroom teacher developed a program called "What I Like." This enabled students to use the multimedia program to express something about themselves, such as "I like pigs." Recording their own voice helped the students build confidence to talk. For example, one student was shy and would seldom speak; she would turn her head away to avoid communication. After working with the program, she opened up and began talking to herself on the computer. The students observed and participated in the activities of those around them, and they were motivated to participate more centrally.

As they gained confidence and experience with the multimedia, the students progressed to producing pictures and voice recordings of every school staff member. This was good for recall because it helped students to recognize people. A social benefit of the computer learning was that it promoted interaction among students. It became a whole-class activity in which students naturally interacted with one another. In the process of working with their teacher and more capable peers, students were able to move from the periphery of the activity to become more centrally involved. Within this classroom, the socially shared cognitions served as a collective zone of proximal development in which students could participate and move toward achievement of their learning potential (Ryba, Selby & Nolan, 1995).

Global InfoLinks: An On-Line Educational Community for Queensland (Australia) Students and Their Teachers

Since the 1980's, Australian schools have been searching for ways to make effective use of computers in the classroom to support the teaching and learning of students. Despite a series of initiatives over the last decade, the use of computers in classrooms is inconsistent and sometimes nonexistent. Likewise, teacher use of computers outside of the classrooms is relatively unsophisticated (Williams, McKeown, Masselos, Stubbs & Potter, 1998). Although much time, energy and money has been spent connecting buildings and local computer networks to the Internet, some of the most promising developments are those that have concentrated on connecting teachers to other teachers. For example, The Global Infolinks (GIL) Project is a series of professional development initiatives throughout Queensland that have adopted a teachers-first approach in supporting teachers in their use of communication technology. The GIL Project showed that an investment in teachers can lead to quality educational and professional activity (Williams, 1995).

The GIL Project recognizes that the best form of support for teachers are their colleagues. In a community of peers, teachers were able to find help for the everyday problems of using technology in educational environments as well as being able to discuss together what it means to be an educator in an increasingly complex world. These peer support communities are based on Lave and Wenger's (1991) concept of communities of practice in that they provide ways for newcomers and old-timers to share the knowledge and practices of the profession and together to share experiences and solve problems about educational issues relating to the use of the Internet. Many teachers are isolated from colleagues and learning opportunities by the fact that they spend the majority of their time working alone in classrooms. However, as Riel (1993) has noted, if we want teachers to provide students with a global perspective, then it is critically important to provide ways of linking teachers to global events and issues as well as to other educators around the world.

The Ipswich City Council (Queensland, Australia) provided all schools in Ipswich with access to the Internet at the beginning of 1995.

The key principles on which the educational Module of GIL was founded include: (a) making decisions that focused on teachers and how teachers would be involved in the project; (b) encouraging teachers to become immersed in the Internet for themselves so they would experience firsthand the impact of this new technology on their lives before they would have to think about the use of this technology in classrooms; (c) reducing barriers to teacher participation by providing hardware and Internet access for teachers; and (d) building a community of participating teachers which had a say in shaping the directions of the GIL Project.

One of the teachers on the GIL Project became involved in training and supporting other teachers as they became involved in using the Internet for personal, professional and curriculum purposes. Her story of "Koala Chris" the travel buddy, provided a good example of how teachers could work together to connect themselves and their students to a global community. Koala Chris was a toy bear who was sent around the world as an ambassador of the classroom. Every day that he was away, Koala Chris sent e-mail messages home and kept a diary of his experiences with children overseas. One of the highlights was when Koala Chris visited NASA and generated so much interest that children tapped into NASA's database of "pre-media" pictures from the Hubble Space Telescope during the Shoemaker Levy Comet collision with Jupiter. Teachers and students had a chance to take a leadership role by hosting many information sessions and tours to share their experiences with the local community of teachers. Through this on-line collaboration, teachers began to understand how they could move from the periphery of activities to becoming skilled contributors to the professional development of teachers in the projects (Blackwell and McKeown, 1995).

By means of data collected from interviews and e-mail of teachers participating in the on-line professional development programs, a shift was noted in the teachers' definitions of the Internet and their attitudes toward it. This was evident in the following comment from a special education teacher:

> After only a few short weeks, I know that my Internet access has changed my perceptions of teaching and learning. The biggest change is my understanding that the Internet provides an opportunity for closer links between professionals. I hope that connections between special education teachers and other teachers in

this way will result in truly inclusive curriculum and practices. I am convinced that students and teachers alike will benefit from the real-life information exchanges and communication experiences unique to e-mail and the Internet. (Williams and KcKeown, 1996)

Global School Psychology Network (GSPN): A Massey University Perspective

The Global School Psychology Network is a professional development community on the Internet for school psychologists and graduate students in school psychology. It is composed of several different sub-communities, referred to as neighborhoods. Each neighborhood has its own private e-mail discussion forum, as well as access to community-wide discussion forums which serve to connect all the participants to one another, regardless of their neighborhood affiliation. One of these neighborhoods was created for students and staff of the Educational Psychology Training Program at Massey University in Auckland, New Zealand. Some of the Program's students live or have internships at a considerable distance from the University. Therefore, it is sometimes difficult to schedule mutually convenient face-to-face meetings. Therefore, an on-line neighborhood of professional practice was created for students and staff. The on-line neighborhood allowed them to communicate at anytime and from any location which has an Internet connection. Graduate students, including internship students, have used the e-mail system to continue class discussions, provide one another with peer support, and consult with professors and supervisors. Also, faculty have used the e-mail system to post and clarify assignments. Massey University faculty and staff believed that the success of their on-line neighborhood would be enhanced if students and faculty had an opportunity to meet face-to-face at an early stage in their graduate studies. This was accomplished through the provision of several on-campus courses during the year.

The GSPN uses a powerful computer messaging system, FirstClass™, which in addition to e-mail discussion groups, provides for live text-based discussions ("chats"), and the development of on-line databases. In addition, all members of the Massey neighborhood had access to an archive of "old messages" exchanged on-line which could be searched by keywords, subject of the message, author or the date on which the message was created. The different resources and discussion areas available to the Massey University members of the GSPN are illustrated in Figure 2 and described in Table 1.

The GSPN also has given Massey students access to colleagues and professional mentors in New Zealand and overseas. By means of the GSPN, students found the answers they needed to assist with their academic work and to help them develop an identity of themselves as professionals. The GSPN provided students with personal support as well as professional consultation. For example, when one capable student announced on-line that she was considering dropping out of graduate studies, messages of support arrived from peers throughout New Zealand. Following consultation with her classmates and many supportive messages, she decided to remain in the Program. Students frequently exchanged ideas about projects and helped one another with brainstorming and problem solving. This was evident in the sharing of ideas about work portfolios which all students were required to assemble as part of the assessment of their progress in the

FIGURE 2. Massey University's Main Computer Screen on the Global School Psychology Network

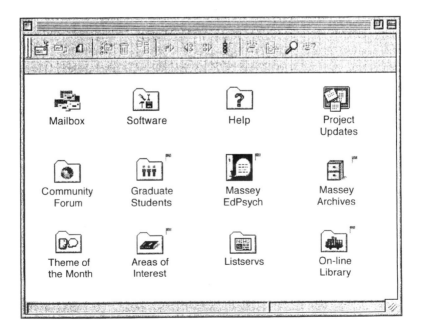

TABLE 1. Folders on Massey University's Main Computer Screen of the Global School Psychology Network

Folder	Description
Mailbox	This folder is for sending private e-mail messages to and receiving messages from individuals. Participants can contact any member of the GSPN by means of this folder.
Software	This folder contains the latest versions of the FirstClass™ software.
Help	This folder provides on-line guidance for using the FirstClass™ messaging system.
Project Updates	This folder contains updates about the GSPN, such as the development of new on-line services.
Community Forum	This folder is for the GSPN participants to communicate with the entire on-line community on a wide range of issues.
Graduate Students	This folder is for all GSPN graduate students. In this area, students provide peer support and problem-solving group assistance to one another.
Massey EdPsych	This folder is for the exclusive use of Massey University graduate students and staff. It is used to communicate about issues related to the Massey's graduate program.
Massey Archives	This folder contains messages from the Massey EdPsych folder that are more then two months old.
Theme of the Month	This folder is accessible to all members of the GSPN. Each month a different topic (e.g., behavior management) is discussed in this folder.
Areas of Interest	This folder contains a database of the interests of the GSPN participants.
Listservs	This folder provides participants with access to school psychology related discussions on the Internet that originate from outside the GSPN.
On-line Library	This folder is reserved for documents such as book reviews and digital materials (e.g., templates of behavioral contracts) that can be downloaded to one's personal computer.

Program. Likewise, when there were questions about assignments, a delegation of students would use the network to ask the university lecturer to provide further information and clarification of requirements. Students also frequently gave each other advice about assessments and interventions for casework. This ready access to peer consultation not only helped to remove the barriers of living and studying in isolation, but provided a range of expertise so that participants could move from the periphery to the center of the learning enterprise.

The Massey University neighborhood became at times a vibrant and active meeting place in which 'newcomers' could be assisted in their learning by communication and involvement with more skilled 'old-timers.' Frequently students began their involvement in the on-line community by reading messages, not making contributions, and observing the on-line interactions. However, when they became sufficiently comfortable with the on-line environment to send a message, they began the move from a novice to experienced on-line user, who would in-turn help other newcomers. The role of a community of practice should be to nurture newcomers so that they gain confidence to move from legitimate peripheral participation to a central place in the community. Conceived in this way, the on-line community is not about transmission of knowledge but about the creation of a professional knowledge network.

After two and one-half months, a formative evaluation was conducted of Massey's graduate students' experience with the GSPN. During this initial period, 17 of Massey's graduate students had joined the GSPN and had sent a total of 279 messages. By means of a questionnaire, 16 of the graduate students rated their experience with respect to several factors, including the extent to which they (a) felt they had become part of a community, (b) felt safe in sending messages, (c) perceived that the GSPN contributed to their professional development, (d) perceived they could influence the direction of the GSPN, and (e) felt supported by the GSPN's participants. The results of the formative evaluation were consistent with aforementioned informal observations. Mean ratings for all factors were above the midpoint of four on their respective seven-point scales (1 = lowest possible rating, 7 = highest possible rating), indicating that the graduate students' initial perceptions about the community were very positive (Kruger & Ryba, 1998). The graduate students gave their highest ratings to the GSPN's safety (5.50, SD = .64), and the lowest ratings to their perceived ability to influence the direction of the GSPN (5.12, SD = .69). Given that these ratings had a relatively narrow range and pertained to a relatively brief period of time, it will be important to compare these data with the students' future reactions to the GSPN.

GUIDELINES FOR THE CREATION OF SUSTAINABLE COMMUNITIES OF PRACTICE

Analysis of projects such as those described here indicate that there are some important underlying principles for the creation of viable and sustainable communities of practice that can enhance cognition and assist with the development of identity and professional knowledge. These principles are:

1. *Active Participation.* Teachers and students need to be active in observing and gathering information and practicing skills as they engage in their professional development activities. By being active learners, newcomers will gain confidence and motivation to move from the periphery to the center of the community activities. For example, newcomers to an on-line community may at first simply observe and read messages but there needs to be a way to encourage their active involvement. This can be facilitated by using a buddy system so that teachers and students have a point of contact within the community.

2. *Guided Learning Opportunities.* Participants in a community of practice need to be provided with guided opportunities to enable them to become immersed in the community. Learning could be assisted by communication and involvement with more skilled people who help determine the activities, level of participation and vision regarding the organization of skills. Effectively, this means placing individuals within their zone of proximal development so that their learning can be enhanced through scaffolding provided by a more capable peer.

3. *Intellectual Collective.* Learning through collaboration with others can have synergistic effects in that the intelligence of the entire community can be raised through shared cognitions and problem solving. The community forms what could be called an "intellectual collective" in which there is the potential for all members to advance their knowledge and skills. The joint problem-solving activities serve as the basis for participants subsequent independent efforts.

4. *Identity Construction.* Socialization into a community of practice not only promotes skill development but also assists in the formation of self identity as a capable practitioner. This inclusive process of generating identities is both a result of and motivation for participation (Lave, 1990). This is evident with students and teachers alike who develop a sense of personal effectiveness through computer-based learning and on-line projects.

5. *Building Cognitive Structures.* Guided participation occurs in the process of individuals interacting informally with one another. It

is through the process of working with their social partners that participants build bridges from their current understanding to reach new understandings through processes inherent in the communications.

6. *Shared Decision Making.* Individuals are more likely to be active participants and take responsibility for maintaining a community when their opinions are highly valued and are taken into consideration when making important decisions about the community's future. Leaders must be willing to unleash the initiative of the participants.

7. *Altruism.* Successful communities have strong norms for helping others. Participants have a positive reciprocity with one another. Individuals believe that helping a peer enriches their experience and increases the likelihood that they also will receive assistance. Underscoring the significance of altruism for a community of practice is the following e-mail message about the GSPN which was sent unsolicited to the third author:

> I initially signed-on to the network expecting to gain knowledge and expertise from other, more experienced professionals. However, months later, to my surprise, . . . I've discovered that I am more often giving feedback and suggestions than I am asking for them. The revelation: Wow, I really know some things! Working in isolation, its easy to forget the skills one has developed. . . . But being on the network has enabled me to recognize the many capabilities I have taken for granted. It's given me a new sense of my strengths and weaknesses, while quieting my self-doubts. My confidence is soaring and, despite the end of the year madness, I'm feeling a level of job satisfaction that I once feared I would never reach.

8. *Psychological Safety.* Professional growth occurs when individuals are willing to take risks and try new approaches to solving old problems. This risk-taking is most likely to occur in communities where the participants have a sense of security that they won't be attacked or belittled because of inexperience or ignorance.

The communities of practice framework provide an encompassing theory for understanding how cultural processes and identity construct and shape one another. The use of the apprenticeship metaphor is relevant for explaining how guided participation enables newcomers to develop in their learning through communication and involvement with relatively more skilled old-timers. Taken together, guided participation within a community of practice ensures the formation of a collective zone of proximal development in which there is the potential for all participants to gain knowledgeable skills through active participation with capable peers. Such a view requires some rethinking about the process of learning, treating it as an emerging property of the whole persons' legitimate peripheral participation in communities of practice. Applied to special education, this framework fits well with the goals of inclusive education to create learning communities in which students and teachers have a sense of belonging and an opportunity to enhance their functioning level through partnerships with others.

REFERENCES

Blackwell, A. & McKeown, L. (1995, December). Pack your bags with travel buddies. *Classroom (Australia)*, pp. 10-13.

Frazer, D., Moltzen, R. & Ryba, K. (1995). *Learners with special needs in Aotearoa New Zealand.* Palmerston North, NZ: Dunmore.

Kruger, L. J. & Ryba, K. (1998). *Massey University's graduate students' experience on the Global School Psychology Network: Formative evaluation.* Unpublished raw data.

Lave, J. (1988). Cognition in Practice: *Mind, mathematics, and culture in everyday life.* Cambridge, UK: Cambridge University Press.

Lave, J. & Wenger, E. (1991). *Situated learning: Legitimate peripheral participation.* Cambridge, UK: Cambridge University Press.

Papert, S. (1980). *Mindstorms: Children, computers and powerful ideas.* New York: Basic Books.

Riel, M. (1993). Global education through learning circles. In L. Harasim (Ed.), *Global Networks: Computers and international communications* (pp. 221-235). Cambridge, MA: MIT Press.

Rogoff, B. (1990). *Apprenticeship in thinking: Cognitive development in social context.* New York: Oxford University Press.

Ryba, K. (1996). Viewing Students as Capable Learners. *Computers in New Zealand Schools, 8 (2),* 3-5.

Ryba, K. & Anderson, B. (1990). *Learning with computers: Effective teaching strategies.* Eugene: International Society for Technology in Education.

Ryba, K., Selby, L. & Nolan, P. (1995). Computers Empower Students With Special Needs. *Educational Leadership, 53 (2),* 82-84.

Vygotsky, L. S. (1987). Thinking and speech (N. Minick, Trans.). In R. W. Rieber and A. S. Carton (Eds.), *The collected works of L.S. Vygotsky* (pp. 37-285). New York: Plenum.

Vygotsky, L. S. (1978). *Mind and society.* Cambridge, UK: Cambridge University Press.

Williams, M., McKeown, L. Masselos, P., Stubbs, J. & Potter, D. (1998). *Global InfoLinks: The story of building an online educational community for Queensland students and their teachers.* Available: http://www.owl.qut.edu.au/qsite/qsite.html

Williams, M. & McKeown, L. (1996). *Professional development model for implementing* internet projects at your school. QSITE Conference CD. Brisbane, Australia: QSITE.

Williams, M. (1995). *Case study of a professional development program conducted in distance* education mode using communications technologies. Masters Thesis, Deakin University.

Using E-Mail to Collaborate
with Professionals and Parents

Gayle Macklem

Manchester (MA) Public Schools

Louis J. Kruger

Northeastern University

Joan Struzziero

Whitman-Hanson Regional School District

SUMMARY. A multidimensional framework of collaboration is provided. We review research on e-mail, and discuss implications for practice and research with respect to collaboration in the schools. We devote particular attention to the implications of e-mail in consulting with classroom teachers, the functioning of school-based teams, and collaborating with parents. Barriers to collaboration are discussed, as well as how e-mail might improve collaboration. Ethical issues in using e-mail are considered, and guidelines for protecting confidentiality are presented. Finally, we discuss possible future uses of the Internet and e-mail with respect to special services in the schools. Examples are provided from our research on e-mail consultation and the Global

---

Address correspondence to: Gayle Macklem, Office of the School Psychologist, Manchester School System, Memorial School, Lincoln Street, Manchester, MA 01944.

The authors express appreciation to the research team of the Global School Psychology Network (GSPN) for their assistance. The GSPN was funded by SoftArc Inc., the Massachusetts School Psychologists Association, the New Jersey Association of School Psychologists, Division 16 of the American Psychological Association, Northeastern University and Massey University.

[Haworth co-indexing entry note]: "Using E-Mail to Collaborate with Professionals and Parents." Macklem, Gayle, Louis J. Kruger, and Joan Struzziero. Co-published simultaneously in *Special Services in the Schools* (The Haworth Press, Inc.) Vol. 17, No. 1/2, 2001, pp. 77-95; and: *Computers in the Delivery of Special Education and Related Services: Developing Collaborative and Individualized Learning Environments* (ed: Louis J. Kruger) The Haworth Press, Inc., 2001, pp. 77-95. Single or multiple copies of this article are available for a fee from The Haworth Document Delivery Service [1-800-342-9678, 9:00 a.m. - 5:00 p.m. (EST). E-mail address: getinfo@haworthpressinc.com].

77

School Psychology Network. *[Article copies available for a fee from The Haworth Document Delivery Service: 1-800-342-9678. E-mail address: <getinfo@haworthpressinc.com> Website: <http://www.HaworthPress.com>]*

KEYWORDS. E-mail, collaboration, consultation, computers

Collaboration has far-reaching significance for education. Educational experts have viewed collaboration as being at the heart of meaningful school improvement efforts (e.g., Friend & Cook, 1992; Idol & West, 1991). Indeed, collaboration is an essential element of many innovative practices, such as teacher teams (Pounder, 1998), school-based management (Idol & West, 1991), building-based school councils (Johnson, 1998), and school-based professional development communities (Louis, Marks, & Kruse, 1996). In regard to special services, collaboration has an obvious and important role in inclusion (Dorsch, 1998), multidisciplinary team assessments (Friend & Cook, 1992), prereferral interventions (Noll, Kamps, & Seaborn, 1993), and consultations with parents and teachers (Nahmias, 1995).

These developments build on an emerging consensus that education has been hindered for too long by the isolated contributions of professionals, and that the complexity of delivering quality education services requires greater interaction among professionals. Collaboration can have an important, albeit indirect, effect on student outcomes (Idol & West, 1991). In a collaborative context, one person's skill or knowledge deficiency can be compensated for by a colleague who has an expertise in that area. Therefore, from a collaborative perspective, each individual's skills are less significant than the combined skills of the group of individuals who are providing the services.

DIMENSIONS OF COLLABORATION

Educational collaboration can be defined as an interactive relationship among co-equal parties who have a common objective (Friend & Cook, 1990). Collaboration implies a partnership in which all participants can potentially benefit. Often, collaboration is structured by a problem solving process. In consultation, for example, the process involves clarifying a problem, designing and implementing an intervention plan, and evaluating the implementation and outcomes.

Collaboration can be characterized by at least four dimensions. One dimension pertains to who the collaborators are. Collaboration can occur between two or more school professionals, school professionals and parents, as well as between school professionals and service providers from other organizations. When special services providers collaborate with general education staff or with individuals who do not work in the schools, it is particularly important for special service providers to understand the perspectives of these other collaborator(s), who may have different expectations. For example, a parent consulting with a school psychologist about his/her child might expect a definitive diagnosis, much like what occurs with a medical problem.

A second dimension of collaboration is the number of the people who are involved. Collaboration can occur in a dyad, a small group, or a large group (Hart, 1998). An example of a large group collaboration is a school's faculty and staff working toward the development of a school-wide community (Smith, 1987). Interagency collaboration is an example of a large group collaboration that might occur between two subgroups (e.g., educators and social services providers) to improve services to students and families (Galvin, 1998; Harvey, 1995). Small and large group collaborative efforts have their respective advantages and disadvantages. For example, although large groups can accomplish more work and can have a wider range of expertise and diversity than smaller groups, they also can be more difficult to coordinate.

A third dimension that can be used to characterize collaboration concerns what is communicated. Individuals communicate on two levels: (a) the content level, which is the overt meaning contained in a verbal message; and (b) the relational level, which pertains to messages about the interpersonal aspects of collaboration. Bales' (1958) seminal work on group process suggested that groups that are able to appropriately balance both the content and interpersonal issues are more likely to attain their tasks.

A fourth dimension relates to the medium of communication. A communication medium can be either synchronous or asynchronous. Synchronous communication occurs when people arrange to communicate at a mutually agreed upon time. Telephone conversations and face-to-face (FTF) meetings are examples of synchronous communication. In contrast, asynchronous communication occurs when people communicate to one another at different times. Asynchronous communication also occurs when individuals write letters, leave messages for one another on answering machines, or send faxes.

These four dimensions coupled with knowledge of the specific organizational context of the collaboration can provide a useful framework for understanding both the practice and research as they relate to the use of e-mail in collaboration. Organizational support and infrastructure seem to have bearing on how successfully e-mail is integrated into people's work. Furthermore, in business settings, there appears to be a positive relationship between adequacy of information technology and the functioning of work teams (Mohrman, Cohen, & Mohrman, 1995). Access to computers and technical support are important elements of this infrastructure.

BARRIERS TO COLLABORATION

As important as collaboration may be, it is difficult to implement in the schools. The nature of schools is such that professionals are often isolated from one another (Hart, 1998). When special services providers meet among themselves or with others, the meeting might be too brief to address the agenda. Indeed, primary barriers to school-based collaboration are time and scheduling constraints (Johnson, 1998). Indeed, the chief reported obstacle to school change (Fullan & Miles, 1992) and implementing teacher assistance teams (Chalfant & Pysh, 1989) is time. Moreover, when a person does have time for a meeting in his/her hectic daily schedule, his/her collaborators might not be available at the same time. As Harvey (1995) notes with respect to interagency collaboration, many school professionals find it easier to meet immediately after school, whereas many mental health professionals are particularly busy at that time.

Space can be another barrier because there are few private meeting rooms in most schools, and the rooms that are available are heavily used. Additional barriers to collaboration in schools include (a) a narrow definition of one's job and student-related responsibilities which preclude collaborative work, (b) lack of training in how to collaborate, (c) strong norms for autonomous work roles, (d) lack of opportunity for follow-up, and (e) a lack of administrative or community support for planning and meeting time (Bondy & Brownell, 1997; Johnson, 1998; Nowacek, 1992).

COMPUTER NETWORKS AS PART OF THE SOLUTION

Computer networks might help lower the barriers to collaboration in schools, including the scheduling of meetings (Teles & Collings,

1995). Computer networks have introduced a new means of asynchronous communication, electronic mail (e-mail). A major advantage of asynchronous communication is that people can collaborate without coordinating when and where they communicate. A major advantage of e-mail in contrast to older means of asynchronous communication (e.g., writing letters) are speed and convenience (Johnson, 1998). E-mail can help sustain interactions which otherwise would be next to impossible to continue. Thus, it is now possible to sustain exchanges when individuals have different schedules and are in different locations (Kollock & Smith, 1998). E-mail can lead to increased communication and information distribution within an organization (Turnage, 1990). Computer networks allow individuals to create a new concept of social space in which individuals can meet and interact with one another. When advanced versions of e-mail programs (e.g., FirstClass™) are used, group collaboration can be supported and enhanced.

REVIEW OF RELEVANT RESEARCH ON E-MAIL

Despite the potential of computer technology for improving collaboration, knowledge about the effects of e-mail on work is in its infancy. Nonetheless, after reviewing the available experimental research on computer-mediated communication, Bordia (1997) concluded that several tentative conclusions are warranted. One of these tentative conclusions is that computer-mediated groups have equaled or exceeded the performance of FTF groups on tasks that involved the generation of ideas. He speculated that there might be fewer blocks to productivity in computer-mediated groups. In contrast to FTF groups, where individuals must wait their turn before sharing an idea, individuals using e-mail can contribute without delay (Strauss & McGrath, 1994). It is not known if the results of these laboratory studies can be generalized to school-based collaborations, such as when people might need to brainstorm alternative intervention strategies for a student. Nevertheless, the results suggest a promising use of e-mail and direct attention toward future research possibilities.

Bordia's (1997) review also suggests that computer-mediated groups seem to have greater equality of participation than do FTF group. Role and social status seem to be less important in regulating participation in computer-mediated groups. Thus, e-mail systems might have the potential to encourage wider and more egalitarian participation within an organization. A similar effect also seemed to occur when another technology, the telephone, was introduced in organizations (Sproull & Kiesler, 1991). E-mail systems might encourage more openness, focusing on the merits of the messages as compared to the status of the sender of the message, and as a result might spawn more egalitarian social structures within organizations (Kollock & Smith, 1996).

E-mail also apparently can provide valuable social support. Dunham, Hurshman, and Litwin (1998) developed a computer network for 42 unmarried mothers with infants. The researchers found a high level of social support and a strong sense of community among the participants. Kruger and Struzziero (1997) with their colleagues developed a computer network for four school psychologists. They also found a high level of cohesion and social support among their on-line group. Kruger and Macklem (1999) found a substantial level of social support among a still larger group: 115 members of a professional development community, The Global School Psychology Network. Despite these positive findings, all of these studies were conducted with homogeneous groups. Therefore, it is not known whether social support would be as evident in heterogeneous groups.

Other research points to apparent limitations of e-mail as a communication medium. As Bordia (1997) noted, computer-mediated groups usually take longer to complete tasks than FTF groups. Moreover, computer-mediated groups can struggle with decisions (e.g., Siegel, Dubrovsky, Kiesler, & McGuire, 1986). Strauss and McGrath (1994) have speculated that these differences might be the result of the simple fact that people can talk more quickly than they can type. In comparison to FTF groups, exchange of information occurs more slowly using computer-mediated communication, and therefore it might be more difficult to complete tasks in a timely manner. In addition, relationships seem to take longer to develop in a computer-mediated environment (Walther, 1995). In spite of the slow beginning, participants in an e-mail group can exhibit solidarity and trust develops after a task has been completed (Walther, 1995).

Bordia (1997) has suggested that misperceptions are more likely in computer-mediated groups. Strauss and McGrath (1994), for example, found that participants in computer-mediated groups were less confident of their comprehension of discussions. The absence of nonverbal and paraverbal cues in e-mail might make it difficult to decipher the precise meaning of a communication, or a person's reaction to a message. Nonverbal communication serves to control the flow of the exchange. Such cues control the smoothness of conversational turns by circumventing long pauses and by signaling the end of exchanges (Trenholm & Jensen, 1992). The lack of social cues also might contribute to the greater apparent occurrence of uninhibited messages in computer-mediated groups as exemplified in aggressive e-mail messages, also referred to as "flames" (e.g., Siegel, Dubrovsky, Kiesler, & McGuire, 1986).

Excessive use of computer-mediated communication also might have negative effects on individuals' personal lives. For example, a longitudinal study (Kraut, Patterson, Lundmark, Kiesler, Mukopadhyay and Scherlis, 1998) found that frequent use of the Internet was related to modest declines in FTF social interaction and psychological well-being. In addition, because the Internet also is becoming a widely used entertainment medium, the use of the Internet for work purposes (especially at home) could lead to the blurring of boundaries between work and entertainment (Kruger & Struzziero, in press). As Braden (1999) has noted, more research needs to be done on the potential unintended and negative effects of Internet use. For example, although special services providers could communicate with parents and other professionals via e-mail during evening hours, it is not clear if this use of e-mail will add to service providers' effectiveness as consultants, and how it might affect the service providers' personal lives.

Overall, the research seems to indicates that e-mail, like any other communication medium, has its strengths and weaknesses. At this time, we are struggling to understand the implications for special services in the schools. Given the nascent state of research on e-mail as well as findings suggestive of important limitations, it seems prudent at this time to view e-mail as complementing and not replacing FTF collaboration. Research and experience suggest that e-mail is well-suited for generating ideas, providing social support, scheduling meetings, and providing updates about cases.

COLLABORATION WITH E-MAIL

Consultation

The most common type of consultation in the schools is client-centered. In client-centered consultation, the consultant provides problem-solving assistance to a consultee, in regard to the consultee's client (Caplan & Caplan, 1993). For example, in a school context, the consultant might be a special services provider, the consultee might be a teacher, and the client might be the teacher's student. Although authors have argued both for (e.g., Friend & Cook, 1992) and against (e.g., Erchul & Chewning, 1990) the importance of collaboration in consultation, some collaborative elements, such as mutual cooperation and rapport, seem important.

Based on the aforementioned e-mail research as well as our own studies (Kruger & Struzziero, 1997; Kruger, Struzziero, Kaplan, Macklem, Poggio, Watts & Weksel, under review), we offer the following tentative guidelines on how e-mail might be combined with FTF consultation. First, e-mail might be used as a means of brainstorming ideas in consultation. For example, after clarification of the student's problem and goal setting but prior to development of an intervention plan, a teacher and a consultant might exchange messages about possible intervention ideas using an e-mail system. However, the research on e-mail also suggests that the consultant and teacher should probably wait for a FTF meeting before deciding on the specific aspects of the intervention plan. For example, the following e-mail exchange (edited for brevity and to protect the anonymity of the participants) occurred during one of our studies:

> *School Psychologist*: . . . I think we're going to have to do much of our consulting with the computer because school time is next to nonexistent. Get back to me with any ideas and or concerns you might have. . . .

> *Teacher*: Mary (the student) confided in me that she would try harder if she didn't have to go to the learning disability room across the hall for reading time. . . . She also complains that she gets yelled at when she doesn't know the answers. I'm not sure that isn't just an excuse. . . .

> *School Psychologist*: . . . The real problem here is the reading. . . . Maybe you could set up a contract with her . . . Make it real specific and set only one or two goals. . . . How does that sound?

> *Teacher*: . . . Let's work on that contract you proposed–great idea! . . . We will meet on Wednesday to discuss procedure. . . . Looking forward to our chat!

This teacher and school psychologist had an intuitive grasp that although e-mail might have an important part in facilitating communication between them, there also was a need for a FTF meeting to work out the details of the intervention.

Using e-mail in consultation also might reduce some teachers' sense of isolation and provide them with a source of social support. In one of our studies (Kruger et al., under review), teachers' ratings of the e-mail messages that they received from their respective consultants (i.e., school psychologists) suggested that the teachers' found the e-mail contact to be very helpful in reducing their sense of professional isolation. We found that three types of content in the messages were related to these ratings: social support (e.g., "I know how upset you must have been."), feedback (e.g., "I liked the way you handled the meeting.") and conceptual information (e.g., "He may have trouble speaking clearly when he is put on the spot.").

Consultation also might be a valuable professional development experience for teachers. In collaborating with school psychologists, they may become more aware of how data collection and systematic reflection might enhance their problem-solving efforts in the classroom. In addition, using e-mail in consultation could be used to expose teachers to new intervention ideas. Indeed, of all the e-mail content categories we examined (Kruger et al., under review), the sharing of conceptual information was the single best predictor of teachers' ratings of the extent to which a message contributed to their knowledge about helping students. Another finding from this study was that school psychologists significantly under predicted the benefits the teachers reported from the e-mail consultation system. One possible interpretation is that without the non-verbal cues it is difficult for the consultant to gauge how much his/her messages are helping the consultee. This possibility also suggests that caution should be exercised in using e-mail to discuss complex issues which might need clarification. This caution is underscored by the following e-mail exchange between a graduate student and the first author. The graduate student was enrolled in the first author's consultation course. The graduate student was reporting his impressions of a meeting between the graduate student's consultee (a teacher) and a student.

Graduate Student: The meeting was short but not unproductive.

Graduate Student's Instructor: Hi Bill. It's discouraging when you put the time and effort in and the student doesn't respond.

In above e-mail exchange, the instructor missed the word "not" in the graduate student's message. As a result, the instructor was offering support for what he thought was an "unproductive meeting," when he should have congratulated the graduate student. This type of misunderstanding might be less likely to occur and easier to clarify in a FTF meeting.

Computer-Mediated Groups and Teams

Peer support groups have been proposed as one solution to the lack of clinical supervision and the need for special services providers to remain current with the ever-evolving knowledge base of one's profession (Kruger & Struzziero, 1997). In addition to the aforementioned social support benefits, Kruger and Struzziero (1997) found that participants of the e-mail peer support group (four school psychologists) indicated that the e-mail messages advanced their knowledge of how to plan and evaluate classroom interventions, as well as how to consult with classroom teachers. Moreover, although the participants had high expectations for what they would learn, ratings indicated that the e-mail experience exceeded their expectations.

If special services providers need to know how to engage in e-mail collaboration, one place to begin to develop that expertise might be in a community of peers. The Global School Psychology Network (GSPN) might serve as such a training site. The GSPN, a professional development community on the Internet, is composed of several different peer support groups (see Ryba, Pine, Mentis, & Bowler, 1999 for a description of the Massey University group). The values of the GSPN (e.g., participants treat one another with the utmost respect) are consistent with the concept of collaboration. The GSPN uses a special type of messaging software, FirstClass™, which not only provides e-mail, but also live chat, on-line biographical sketches, and database features. Ratings from the participants indicated a high level of satisfaction of the GSPN with respect to professional development (Kruger & Macklem, 1999). Moreover, 41 percent of the respondents indicated that the GSPN was one of the best professional development experiences that they had during the year of the study (Kruger & Macklem, 1999). Despite this positive finding, many unresolved issues exist. For example, is there an optimal size for an on-line peer support group? Will common group problems, such as one member monopolizing the discussion, also occur with on-line groups?

Collaboration with Parents

Collaboration between home and school is a reciprocal process that takes place over time, incorporates frequent communication, and is characterized by respect between parents and school staff (Nahmias, 1995). From a historical perspective, Henry (1996) has noted that as state-provided education became the mode in the United States parents tended to become less involved with schools, especially in regard to important decision making. Schools were not being built around the integrated school-community concept, and as a consequence were more distant from their respective communities. However, this trend might be reversing because parent-school collaboration is now viewed as an important part of school reform (see, e.g., Henry, 1996). Parent-school collaboration also can provide resources to and support for schools, making schools more responsive to community needs. In addition, parent-school collaboration can help parents access information about their children's academic progress. Parent involvement is a sufficiently high priority in some large school systems that individuals are hired for the express purpose of facilitating parent involvement and communication. Systematic investigation on the effects of home-school collaboration is relatively new. However, the research that has been done is promising. For example, parent involvement seems to be an important factor in promoting student learning for both boys and girls, as well as for students from different ethnic backgrounds (Keith, Keith, Quirk, Sperduto, Santillo & Killings, 1998).

Increased home-school collaboration should be a particularly important priority for special services providers. Although most parents might benefit from communication with school professionals, families with handicapped children have particular needs for collaboration (Nahmias, 1995). Collaboration, for example, might help families cope with the stress associated with having a child with a learning problem. Davern (1996) believes that parents of children with special needs should have regular communication with one individual at school who knows their child and his or her learning needs.

E-mail might have a role in making home-school collaboration more of a reality because a traditional barrier to collaboration has been the difficulty in finding a mutually convenient meeting time. Christenson (1995) argued that successful partnerships between special services providers and parents need to be responsive to parents' schedules and should use a variety of communication methodologies. As important as FTF interactions between school professionals and parents might be, special services providers work under serious time constraints. E-mail also might be an important means of providing individualized attention to parental concerns and needs. Wise (1995), for example, has stressed the importance of school psychologists spending time with parents away from other school staff so that parents will view school psychologists as advocates for their child. Indeed, e-mail could increase the frequency of contact between home and school.

Given the potential for e-mail to overcome the scheduling barrier to home-school collaboration, it seems unfortunate that we could not locate research on the use of e-mail in home-school collaboration. Nonetheless, there are examples of how technology might be used to foster greater home-school collaboration. Automated telephone messaging systems and voice mail, for instance, have been used by teachers to inform parents of topics covered in school and homework assignments. A common use of the Internet is to publish students' work (see, e.g., Kristovich, Hertzog, & Klein, 1997). However, it is not clear how this is an improvement over children taking their work home to show their parents. Although new software has been developed to exploit the world-wide web's potential to involve parents in their students' education (see, e.g., http://www.edulinksys.com), the evaluations of these efforts need to be strengthened.

ETHICAL ISSUES

As special services providers begin to incorporate the use of e-mail and other computer-related technologies into their daily work, they need to be mindful of the risks as well as the benefits of these new technologies. Access to computer technology is proceeding at a rate faster than are theory, research and ethical guidelines about its use. The pace of development is so fast that Harvey and Kruger (1998), for example, argued that ethical guidelines have not kept pace with the advancement of computer-mediated communication.

The first step in responsible e-mail use for professional purposes is to understand the limitations of the medium, including the aforementioned research. Many of the uses of e-mail suggested by us require a secure e-mail system as well as users who understand how to avoid breeches in privacy. At present, most of the e-mail sent over the

Internet is vulnerable to being read by unintended audiences. However, there are highly secure alternatives, referred to groupware and intranets. These alternatives use software that provides at least two levels of security beyond typical e-mail: (a) storage of e-mail on a secure computer (i.e., server) which limits or prohibits people, who do not have authorized accounts, from sending messages to the e-mail system; and (b) the use of encryption. Many e-mail messages are relayed across multiple computers (i.e., servers) before the messages reach their final destination. At each relay point, messages are vulnerable to interception by sophisticated computer users. To combat piracy of messages, encryption schemes have been developed. An encryption scheme scrambles the message when it is transit and puts it back together when the message reaches its destination. However, encryption requires that both the sender and receiver use the same encryption scheme. At present, encryption is still not widely used. Unencrypted e-mail is as seductive and dangerous as is talking about students in the teacher's lounge at one's school. Special services providers are obligated to learn how secure their e-mail system is, who might have access to their messages, and how to protect important or confidential information.

Technology alone will not maintain the confidentiality of e-mail messages. Indeed, individuals also need to be alert to the possible ways in which they themselves might inadvertently compromise e-mail security. Much like the types of careless errors that can occur with paper documents, such as leaving a confidential file on a desk, careless errors can occur with e-mail. For example, a user might inadvertently save his/her password from an e-mail account on a computer that others have access to. However, because of the novelty of the technology, special services providers might be less alert to potential security risks with e-mail, such as sending a confidential message to the wrong person. In addition, even when messages are contained within a local e-mail system and encrypted, the local computer administrator and his/her assistants often have access to these messages. The importance of confidentiality issue will undoubtedly mushroom as more special services providers use e-mail for professional purposes.

In addition to the ethical issues, there might be legal implications to discussing student cases via e-mail. E-mail, for example, has been subpoenaed as evidence in court cases (Brown, 1999). Moreover, unlike paper records, e-mail records can be difficult to destroy. Administrators of e-mail systems often maintain back-up files. Furthermore, companies are now specializing in the recovery of information from digital storage media (e.g., the hard disk of an individual's personal computer) which users thought was erased. The cautious approach would be to avoid writing anything in an e-mail message that the sender would not feel comfortable defending in a public forum.

Training as well as information dissemination also can be used to combat the misuse of e-mail for collaborative purposes. Information dissemination can fail simply because people did not read a school system's guidelines for e-mail use. School systems need to commit the time and money to do adequate training. In addition to formal training of all users, intensive training can be done with specific individuals, who then can model appropriate use of the e-mail system. The GSPN uses this latter approach by assigning a facilitator to each on-line discussion area.

POSSIBLE FUTURE USES OF THE INTERNET AND E-MAIL IN COLLABORATION

Bauch (1997) has advocated the use of multiple types of communication technologies for the purpose of creating what he has refereed to as a "transparent school," where the time, scheduling, and technical barriers between school and home would virtually disappear. In this context, e-mail becomes one of many useful means of communicating important general and as well as personalized information to parents and students. Parents of students, who are being educated at home or are home bound due to illness, might particularly benefit from the use of e-mail to stay in contact with school professionals.

E-mail is the mere beginning of a communications revolution driven by advances in digital information technology, mobile devices, and the Internet. This revolution will free special services providers from the shackles of time and place, and bring them closer to collaborating with others at any time and from any place. In addition, there will be a bewildering array of communication choices: (a) FTF meetings, (b) telephone, (c) voice mail, (d) e-mail, and (e) live and recorded video. Collaborations that seem daunting now may soon become commonplace. For example, despite the empirical support for conjoint consultation (Sheridan, 1997), there are often practical barriers to its implementation. Chief among these is finding a mutually convenient meeting time for three or more individuals. A working parent might only be available in the evening; the time period that is most inconvenient for the consultant and teacher. By means of a video-conference over the Internet, a teacher and school psychologist could meet together at school and be joined by a parent from his/her work-place during the parent's lunch break. E-mail in combination with video-conferencing might make it easier to facilitate the implementa-tion of interventions across both school and home environments.

Local e-mail systems can be used to facilitate communication among members of educational teams, and provide common access to minutes from meetings and progress reports, as well as provide fol-low-up discussions about cases. As Huebner and Gould (1991) have noted, the lack of follow-up on recommendations continues to be a concern with multidisciplinary teams. Team meetings might become more efficient when members can instantly disseminate pre-meeting notes and construct a meeting agenda on-line. A major problem in assessing many students' behavioral difficulties is understanding the relationship between home environment and the student's behavioral problems. As the Internet becomes capable of transmitting larger chunks of digital information, it will soon be practical to send digital video over the Internet. Thus, it will be possible for parents to make a video recording of their child's behavior at home and immediately send it to a special services provider. Similarly, the school will be able to send video to the parents as well. Retrospective accounts of behav-ior and successful intervention strategies could be replaced by audio-visual data. Of course, it would be important to resolve consent and privacy issues in sharing any audio or video data.

Collaborations also can provide a context for providing feedback to special services providers. Collaborators often develop a clear under-standing of one another's contributions to case or work-related prob-lems. Therefore, there would seem to be ample opportunity to com-ment on fellow collaborators' performances. For example, a teacher might note the practical implications of a speech therapist's assess-ment report. Unfortunately, the limited research done on e-mail among school professionals, suggests that they rarely use it to provide feed-back (Kruger et al., under review; Kruger, Cohen, Marca, & Mat-thews, 1996). Future research should address the barriers to sharing feedback via e-mail and what can be done to overcome them.

As technology provides special services providers with more freedom to decide how and when they will do their work, there needs to be commensurate progress in knowledge and responsibility. At present, few guidelines and research studies are available. It is imperative that we understand the strengths and weaknesses of emerging communication technologies before they become ubiquitous. For example, consultants should understand how e-mail is different than FTF meetings before they use the technology. Delay of this type of research incurs the risk that technologies will be misused. In tackling this research agenda, special services providers will need to move outside of their own narrow specialties and become more conversant with research in other disciplines, such as communication and decision-making that have a tradition of illuminating the relationship between people and technology. We hope that this article has not only pointed to the practical issues involved in e-mail use, but also provided directions for such systematic research. E-mail will be part of the work world of special services providers for the foreseeable future.

REFERENCES

Bales, R. F. (1958). Task roles and social roles in problem solving groups. In E. E. Maccoby, T. M. Newcomb, & E. L. Hartley (Eds.), *Readings in social psychology (3rd ed.)*. New York: Holt, Rinehart, & Winston.

Bauch, J. P. (1997, September). *Dialogue and Communication between School and Home.* Paper presented at the Education is a Dialogue and Democracy Conference, Bielawa, Poland. (ERIC Document Reproduction Service No. ED 416 981).

Bondy, E., & Brownell, M. T. (1997). Overcoming barriers to collaboration among partners-in-teaching. *Intervention in School and Clinic, 33* (2), 112-115.

Bordia, P. (1997). Face-to-face versus computer-mediated communication: A synthesis of the experimental literature. *The Journal of Business Communication, 34* (1), 99-121.

Braden, J. (1999). Discussant of symposium. In J. Cummings (Chair), *How will the Internet change worldwide communities of practice and training in school psychology?* Symposium conducted at the Annual Convention of the National Association of School Psychologists, Las Vegas, Nevada.

Caplan, G. & Caplan, R. (1993). *Mental health consultation and collaboration.* San Francisco: Jossey-Bass.

Brown, A. J. (1999, January). E-mail and confidentiality. *Massachusetts Psychologist, 6* (11), 5.

Chalfant, J. C., & Pysh, M. V. (1989). Teacher assistance teams: Five descriptive studies on 96 teams. *Remedial and Special Education, 10,* 49-58.

Christenson, S. L. (1995). Families and schools: What is the role of the school psychologist? *School Psychology Quarterly, 10,* 118-132.

Davern, L. (1996). Listening to parents of children with disabilities. *Educational Leadership, 53* (7), 61-63.

Dorsch, N.G. (1998). *Community, collaboration, and collegiality in school reform: An odyssey toward connections.* Albany, NY: State University of New York Press.

Dunham, P. J., Hurshman, A., & Litwin, E. (1998). Computer-mediated social support: Single young mothers as a model system. *American Journal of Community Psychology, 26,* 281-306.

Erchul, W. P., & Chewning, T. G. (1990). Behavioral consultation from a request-centered relational communication perspective. *School Psychology Quarterly, 5,* 1-20.

Friend, M., & Cook, L. (1992). *Interactions: Collaboration skills for school professionals.* New York: Longman.

Friend, M. & Cook, L. (1990). Collaboration as a predictor of success in school reform. *Journal of Educational and Psychological Consultation, 1*(1), 69-86.

Fullan, M & Miles, M. (1992). Getting Reform Right: What Works and What Doesn't. *Phi Delta Kappan, 73,* 745-752.

Galvin, P. F. (1998). The organizational economics of interagency collaboration. In Pounder, D. G. (Ed.), *Restructuring Schools for Collaboration: Promises and Pitfalls* (pp. 43-63). Albany, NY: State University of New York Press.

Hart, A. W. (1998). Marshaling forces: Collaboration across educator roles. In Pounder, D. G. (Ed.), *Restructuring Schools for Collaboration: Promises and Pitfalls* (pp. 89-120). Albany, NY: State University of New York Press.

Harvey, V. S. (1995). Interagency collaboration. Providing a system of care for students. *Special Services in the Schools, 10* (1), 165-181.

Harvey, V. S., & Kruger, L. J. (1998, March). Computer-mediated consultation: Ethical issues and guidelines. *Communiqué, 26* (6), pp. 6, 8, 10, 12.

Henry, M. E. (1996). *Parent-School Collaboration: Feminist organizational structures and school leadership.* Albany, NY: State University of New York Press.

Huebner, E. S., & Gould, K. (1991). Multidisciplinary teams revisited: Current perceptions of school psychologists regarding team functioning. *School Psychology Review, 20,* 428-434.

Idol, L., & West, J. (1991). Educational collaboration: A catalyst for effective schooling. *Intervention in School and Clinic, 27* (2), 70-78.

Johnson, B. J. (1998). Organizing for collaboration: A reconsideration of some basic organization principles. In D. G. Pounder (Ed.), *Restructuring Schools for Collaboration: Promises and Pitfalls* (pp. 9-25). Albany, NY: State University of New York Press.

Keith, T. Z., Keith, P. B., Quirk, K. J., Sperduto, J., Santillo, S., & Killings, S. (1998). Longitudinal effects of parent involvement on high school grades: Similarities and differences across gender and ethnic groups. *Journal of School Psychology, 36*(3), 335-363.

Kollock, P., & Smith, M. (1996). Managing the virtual commons: Cooperation and conflict in computer communities. In Herring, S. (Ed.), *Computer-Mediated Communication: Linguistic, Social, and Cross-Cultural Perspectives* (pp. 109-128). Amsterdam: John Benjamins.

Kraut, R., Patterson, M., Lundmark, V., Kiesler, S., Mukopadhyay, T., & Scherlis, W.

(1998) Internet paradox: A social technology that reduces social involvement and psychological well-being? *American Psychologist, 53*, 1017-1031.

Kristovich, Hertzog, & Klein (1997, October). *Connecting Families through Innovative Technology in an Early Childhood Gifted Program.* Proceedings of the Families, Technology, and Education Conference, Chicago, IL. (ERIC Document Reproduction Service No. ED 425 019).

Kruger, L. J., Cohen, S., Marca, D., & Matthews, L. (1996). Using the Internet to extend training in team problem solving. *Behavior Research Methods, Instruments and Computers, 28*(2), 248-252.

Kruger, L. J., & Macklem, G. (1999, April). The Global School Psychology Network. In J. Cummings (Chair), *How will the Internet change worldwide communities of practice and training in school psychology?* Symposium conducted at the Annual Convention of the National Association of School Psychologists, Las Vegas, Nevada.

Kruger, L. J. Struzziero, J. A. Kaplan, S., Macklem, G., Poggio, B., Watts, R., & Weksel, T. (1998). *Computer-Mediated Consultation: Perceptions of Consultee Outcomes.* Manuscript submitted for publication.

Kruger, L. J., & Struzziero, J. A. (1997). Computer-mediated peer support of consultation: Case description and evaluation. *Journal of Educational and Psychological Consultation, 8* (1), 75-90.

Kruger, L. J. & Struzziero, J. (in press). Using the Internet for consultation, peer support, and supervision. To appear in A. Bordas (Ed.), *Technological innovations and the school psychologist.* Bethesda, MD: National Association of School Psychologists.

Louis, K. S., Marks, H. M., & Kruse, S. (1996). Teachers' professional community in restructuring schools. *American Educational Research Journal, 33* 757-798.

Mohrman, S. A., Cohen, S. G., Mohrman, A. M. Jr. (1995). Designing Team-Based Organizations: New Forms for Knowledge Work. San Francisco: Jossey-Bass Publishers.

Nahmias, M. L. (1995). Communication and collaboration between home and school for students with ADD. *Intervention in School and Clinic, 30*, 241-247.

Noll, M. B., Kamps, D., & Seaborn, C. F. (1993). Prereferral intervention for students with Emotional or Behavioral Risks: Use of a behavioral consultation model. *Journal of Emotional and Behavioral Disorders, 1*, 203-214.

Nowacek, E. J. (1992). Professionals talk about teaching together: Interviews with five collaborating teachers. *Intervention in School and Clinic, 27*, 262-276.

Pounder, D. G. (1998). Teacher teams: Redesigning teacher's work for collaboration. In Pounder, D. G. (Ed.). *Restructuring Schools for Collaboration: Promises and Pitfalls* (pp. 65-88). Albany: State University of New York Press.

Ryba, K, Pine, T., Mentis, M. & Bowler, J. (1999). Training educational psychologists for the 21st century: A Massey University perspective. *The Bulletin of the New Zealand Psychological Society, 95*, 5-13.

Sheridan, S. M. (1997). Conceptual and empirical bases of conjoint behavioral consultation. *School Psychology Quarterly, 12*, 119-133.

Siegel, J., Dubrovsky, V., Kiesler, S., & McGuire, T. (1986). Group processes in computer-mediated communication. *Organizational Behavior and Human Decision Processes, 37,* 157-187.

Smith, S. C. (1987). The collaborative school takes shape. *Educational Leadership, 45* (3), 4-6.

Sproull, L. & Kiesler, S. (1991). *Connections: New ways of working in the networked organization.* Cambridge, MA: MIT Press.

Strauss, S. G., & McGrath, J. E. (1994). Does the medium matter? The interaction of task type and technology on group performance and member reactions. *Journal of Applied Psychology, 79,* 87-95.

Teles, L. & Collings, T. (1995). Virtual experiments and group tasks in a web-based collaborative course in introductory electronic communication. In Mohrman, S. A., Cohen, S. G., & Mohrman, Jr., A. M. (Eds.), *Designing Team-Based Organizations: New Forms for Knowledge Work* (pp. 399-400). San Francisco CA: Jossey-Bass Publishers.

Trenholm, S., & Jensen, A. (1992). *Interpersonal Communication (2nd ed.),* Belmont, CA: Wadsworth Publishing Company.

Turnage, J. J. (1990). The challenge of new workplace technology for psychology. *American Psychologist, 45,* 171-178.

Walther, J. B. (1995). Relational aspects of computer-mediated communication: Experimental observations over time. *Organization Science, 6,* 186-203.

Wise, P. S. (1995). Communicating with parents. In Thomas, A. & Grimes, J. (Eds.), *Best Practices in School Psychology-III* (pp. 279-287). Washington, DC: The National Association of School Psychologists.

Family and Related Service Partnerships in Home Computer Decision-Making

Howard P. Parette
Cindy L. Anderson

Southeast Missouri State University

SUMMARY. Effective home computer decision-making often requires partnerships between families from different cultures and professionals. This article provides a review of literature related to perceptions of home computers held by various cultural groups. A case is made that families vary in their *degree of involvement* in working with professionals to make decisions about home computers. A discussion is provided related to expectations that families may have of professionals who work with them during team decision-making processes. Because families also vary markedly with regard to *supports needed* to ensure effective implementation of home computers, *training* is described as a primary support required by many families. *[Article copies available for a fee from The Haworth Document Delivery Service: 1-800-342-9678. E-mail address: <getinfo@haworthpressinc.com> Website: <http://www.HaworthPress.com>]*

KEYWORDS. Family partnerships, collaboration, computers at home

The importance of family partnerships with related services personnel in the development of individualized education plans (IEPs) has

Address correspondence to: Dr. Howard P. Parette, Department of Elementary and Special Education, College of Education, Southeast Missouri State University, One University Plaza, Cape Girardeau, MI 63701-4799.

This article is supported in part by Grant No. H029K50072 from the U.S. Department of Education. Opinions expressed herein are those of the authors alone and should not be interpreted to have agency endorsement.

[Haworth co-indexing entry note]: "Family and Related Service Partnerships in Home Computer Decision-Making." Parette, Howard P., and Cindy L. Anderson. Co-published simultaneously in *Special Services in the Schools* (The Haworth Press, Inc.) Vol. 17, No. 1/2, 2001, pp. 97-113; and: *Computers in the Delivery of Special Education and Related Services: Developing Collaborative and Individualized Learning Environments* (ed: Louis J. Kruger) The Haworth Press, Inc., 2001, pp. 97-113. Single or multiple copies of this article are available for a fee from The Haworth Document Delivery Service [1-800-342-9678, 9:00 a.m. - 5:00 p.m. (EST). E-mail address: getinfo@haworthpressinc.com].

been well-documented in the professional literature for several decades (Berger, 1981; Simpson, 1996; Stainback & Stainback, 1990; Turnbull & Turnbull, 1978). Operationally, a family-professional partnership refers to an association between a family and one or more professionals that functions collaboratively, using agreed upon roles in pursuit of a common interest (Dunst & Paget, 1991). Through such partnerships, opportunities are created *for all partners* to become empowered to make informed decisions about the best course of action to achieve a common goal or interest (Judge & Parette, 1998). These partnerships are particularly important when assistive technology devices are being considered by decision-making teams (Ainsa, Murphy, Thouvenelle, & Wright, 1994; Beaver & Mann, 1994; Parette & Brotherson, 1996; Parette, Hourcade, & VanBiervliet, 1993). As defined in P.L. 105-17, the *Individuals with Disabilities Education Act Amendments of 1997* (IDEA), assistive technologies include a range of items, pieces of equipment, or product systems that may be used to increase, maintain, or improve the functional abilities of children with disabilities [20 U.S.C. 1401, §602(1)].

Home computers are one type of assistive technology devices often recommended by IEP teams. Support for home computer usage was reflected in a policy statement on assistive technology issued in 1991 by the Office of Special Education Programs (OSEP) (RESNA Technical Assistance Project, 1992). Basically, OSEP's position was that students must be provided with *home access* to assistive technology if a team decided that it would help the child to benefit from a free and appropriate public education (FAPE).

Generally speaking, professionals have advocated for children having access to computers at both home *and* school to maximize their learning potential (Debenham & Smith, 1994; Fullerton, 1995; Male, 1994; Ullery, 1993). When working with children with disabilities and families from different cultural backgrounds, the operational assumptions which guide team decision-making for children from Euro-American backgrounds may not be appropriate (Soto, Huer, & Taylor, 1997). For example, values such as competition, the importance of education, individual initiative, and commitment to a cure for the child's learning problems–important Euro-American values–may not be shared by children and families from other cultural backgrounds. Many families want to be actively involved, while others will choose to have minimal or no involvement. This may also be true of involvement with home computers.

Before decisions are made regarding selection and provision of computer systems for home use by children and families, consideration must be given to both family and cultural issues (Brotherson, Cook, & Parette, 1996; Hourcade, Parette, & Huer, 1997; Scherer, 1996). To make decisions otherwise could potentially result in lack of family involvement in planning, inappropriate computer recommendations, and adverse effects on the child and family (Parette & Angelo, 1998; Scherer, 1996). As Ullery (1993) noted, "Assuming reasons why parents are not participating is a serious error on the part of school staff members. Understanding the priorities, needs, cultural differences, and concerns of parents are of critical importance in planning . . . " (pp. 49-50).

This article explores a range of issues related to the development of effective family and related service personnel partnerships related to home computer decision-making. Specifically, the following questions will be addressed:

1. Do families of children with disabilities across cultures differ in their perceptions of and need for home computers?
2. Do families have expectations of professionals while making a decision to buy a computer?
3. Can specific supports enable related service personnel to more effectively work in partnership with families to provide home computers to children with disabilities?

REVIEW OF LITERATURE

Computer Usage Across Cultures

Usage of home computers increases markedly each year, suggesting that any estimates of actual usage are underestimates. Almost one-third of U.S. households have been reported to have personal computers (Charp, 1996), and ownership appears to be related to socioeconomic status and educational level. Debenham and Smith (1994) noted that approximately 75% of middle class now have computers, while only about 11% of households with incomes less than $20,000 have personal computers (Times Mirror Center for the People and the Press,

1994). The majority of families buying home computers are concerned with their children's education and home learning (Brady, 1993; Charp, 1996). Families of younger children tend to see use of home computers as a means to develop social and emotional abilities rather than cognitive skills, while parents of older children view computers as tools to build social, emotional and cognitive skills equally (Hutinger, 1994).

Not surprisingly, home computer usage is significantly influenced by both SES and cultural variables (Resta, 1992). Euro-American students tend to have computers in their home environments more frequently than children from Hispanic, African and Native American children (Educational Testing Center, 1985). Lower income families are less likely to have computers than middle and upper income families. More computers are provided to middle and upper income children in the schools (Cole & Griffin, 1987). Differences in computer distribution may be more frequently attributable to student computer competence or access to appropriate computer experiences (Educational Testing Center, 1985). Certainly, issues regarding equity of school resources have also arisen regarding home usage of computers (Inge & Shepherd, 1995; Lockard, Abrams, & Many, 1997; Resta, 1995). Milone and Salpeter (1996) observed that just as budgetary constraints have widened the gaps between the haves and have-nots, so too may technology in the home. Piller (1992) found that children and teachers in impoverished school districts are less likely to have computers in their homes. However, as Shashaani (1994) noted, *parental attitudes* played a greater role in student interest in home computers than did SES.

Early efforts to provide computers to families in communities have been equivocal. For example, Kitabachi (1987) reported on the impact of home computers provided to 5th grade African-American students. After approximately 10 hours of training to help them use an Apple computer in the home, families reported favorable perceptions of their experiences and the importance of the computer as a learning tool for their children. Follow-ups of these students in the 6th grade reflected consistently high parental perception of the importance of home computers (Ross, Smith, Morrison et al., 1989). Based on implementation of a community-based computer information system, Trachtman, Spirek, Sparks, and Stohl (1991) reported that even though families acknowledge the importance of computers, certain factors must be considered before integrating them into the home. These include (a) an understanding of advantages of the computer, (b) compatibility of the computer with family value and belief systems, (c) complexity of the computer, (d) degree to which family members may experiment with the computer, and (e) extent to which others may see the results of home usage of the computer. Just as important is the provision of training and related supports to ensure the success of the computer in the home setting (Parette, 1997). For example, in New Mexico, great progress has been demonstrated in providing families of Native American children with computers for home usage via the Take Home Computer Program (Fullerton, 1995). Approximately 200 computers are distributed to families on a 10-week rotation basis, and there is reliance on self-paced lessons that are text-based and which are supplemented with home enrichment activities. As noted by Fullerton (1995), the program was designed to "enable parents to contribute to their children's success in school" (p. 19). The assumption is that parents *want to become involved* in their children's education, or *are capable to participate.* As noted previously, this assumption may be flawed as families may lie along a continuum, ranging from little or no interest in participating to total involvement in their children's education. This willingness to participate will be influenced by a range of factors, including (a) family values, (b) cultural influences, (c) computer enculturation (i.e., the degree to which families have been influenced by outside forces regarding the importance of computers, or their past experiences in using computers), and (d) mainstream forces (e.g., increasing use of the Internet).

Family values. Some families may see computers as a panacea, rather than tools (Swartz, 1993). To be most effective, Hutinger (1994) noted that assistive technology applications must be planned to help them achieve specific goals and must be implemented as tools to accomplish targeted goals. Related service personnel are also guilty of emphasizing the technology itself, rather than the role changes or "social envelope" required to implement the technology (Tornatsky, 1983, p. 7). Use of home computers for learning requires new role behaviors on the part of children, and new interaction patterns between children and family members (Giacquinta & Lane, 1990). They are innovations for many families, and thus must be evaluated against criteria for any innovation: (a) family member receptiveness to the computer, (b) family willingness/ability to implement the computer,

(c) availability of support resources, and (d) compatibility of the family system with the computer (Gross, Giacquinta, & Bernstein, 1971). Rogers (1983) suggested that other important factors include the family's perceived awareness of the computer and perceived need for it. It is noteworthy that not all families will be receptive to provision of a home computer, particularly if changes in routines and additional stressors (e.g., repeated training) are introduced or made aware initially to the family prior to purchase (Hourcade et al., 1997).

Cultural factors. Culture may be seen as a "lens" through which families view the world (Battle, 1993). In the process of building partnerships with families, related service personnel may find that family members from non-Euro-American backgrounds have markedly different lenses through which their world is viewed. Thus, it is inappropriate for school personnel to assume that families of children with disabilities from all cultural backgrounds have the same reasons for becoming involved in the education of their children (Klimes-Dougan, Lopez, Nelson, & Adelman, 1992).

Differences may be seen in perceptions of disability held by family members (Groce & Zola, 1993), attitudes toward the education system (Harry, Allen, & McLaughlin, 1995), priorities regarding services deemed important for the child and family (Soto et al., 1997), ideas regarding the importance and process of childcare (Anderson & Fenichel, 1989; Ogbu, 1987), family perceptions of their ability to collaborate with professionals (Harry et al., 1995), and the extent to which life circumstances are viewed as being overwhelming (Rosado, 1994).

Computer enculturation. Families will vary with regard to their perceptions of the need for and usefulness of computers. These perceptions are influenced by many factors, including the media and past experiences with technology. Children with disabilities and their families have increasingly been subjected to the media "presence" of computers (e.g., television programming, radio, movies). The growing visibility of the Internet and the importance of home computers for accessing and using information has also been felt by many families.

Past experiences in using computers are also powerful influences on the family's willingness to use home computers; if experiences have been positive, it is reasonable to expect that families will be receptive to their use. Conversely, if the family has had negative experiences in using computers in the past, their perceptions may be quite different. School exposure to computers, which is closely linked to socioeconomic status and computer resources in schools, has a powerful impact on the perceptions that some cultural groups have toward computers (Carver, 1995).

Mainstream forces. A range of external forces in our society may also have varying degrees of effect on families of children with disabilities. For example, ongoing reports have noted that our culture has become increasingly dependent on technology and that skilled workers will be needed to a greater extent than in decades past (Lee, 1997; Office of Technology Policy, 1997). Greater family empowerment, fueled to a large extent by passage of the *Americans with Disabilities Act of 1990* (P.L. 102-119) and subsequent advocacy training nationwide, has resulted in greater numbers of families feeling empowered to advocate for the computer needs of their children (Wehman, 1993).

Family Expectations of Team Members

It has been noted that professional and family perceptions of educational interventions needed for children with disabilities can vary markedly (Hutinger 1994). With regard to assistive technology, it may be anticipated that such differences in perspectives also exist (Kemp, 1998; Parette et al., 1996). Conversations with family members from around the country regarding electronic communication devices and computers have indicated that families have very specific expectations of related service personnel–expectations which may differ greatly from professional expectations of family members (Parette et al., 1996). Based on such expectations, team members should ask a variety of questions during home computer decision-making (see Table 1).

PARTNERSHIPS WITH FAMILIES: TWO CASE STUDIES

The importance of considering family, cultural, enculturation and mainstream forces during home computer decision-making with families cannot be overemphasized. The following two scenarios represent actual occurrences in which related service personnel were involved in planning for computer implementation in the home setting.

Scenario 1: The Case of Adam

Adam was a second grade student with learning disabilities. He was being considered for placement into the multicategorical resource room. His father was a farmer and his mother worked as a nurse in a

TABLE 1. Factors and Team Questions Related to Home Computer Usage by Children with Disabilities and Their Families

Factor	Team Questions
Child	• Does the child have the requisite skills (with or without accommodations) to effectively use the computer? • Will child preferences for peripherals and adaptations be considered? • Does the child want to use the computer in the home? • Is the child willing to receive training and other supports necessary to effectively use the computer?
Computer	• Are the features of the computer system (with or without adaptations) compatible with the child's skills and abilities? • Will training and other supports be required to effectively use the computer? • Will opportunities be provided for hands-on experiences with the computer prior to implementation in the home?
School	• Are resources available for purchase and support of the computer in the home? • Will school personnel be required to provide training (in the native language when appropriate) to the child and family members in the home? • What are the targeted educational goals for the child's use of the computer at home? • Will the computer be protected from theft and damage? • Have options been considered for replacement of the computer during repair intervals?
Family	• Does the family want a computer in the home setting? • If so, is computer usage congruous with family needs and goals? • Will changes in family routines and responsibilities result from use of the home computer? • Are families willing and able to accept these changes? • Will siblings have access to the computer? • Will training and supports (in the native language when appropriate) be provided for effective use of the computer in the home?
Cultural	• Does the family (both immediate and extended) feel that the child's use of computers is important? • Will use of the computer draw unnecessary or negative attention to the child? • Will use of the computer increase the child's opportunities for interactions in the community?

hospital. The parents attended all the activities of their five children and were involved in their children's academic work.

Adam's parents knew early in first grade that school was a struggle for Adam. They provided assistance to Adam, making them aware of the difficulties he had with reading and writing. They agreed that Adam should be referred for special services because of his learning disabilities. They sought out information on learning disabilities and recognized those characteristics in their son. However, on the school assessments, Adam failed to qualify for special education. This led his parents to seek out university assessment services. The university diagnosed Adam as learning disabled but because of his prior school assessment scores, the school's IEP team would not agree to place Adam into the learning disabilities program. For a year and a half, the parents continued to push for placement but assessment scores continued to disqualify Adam.

The following year, Adam had difficulty in second grade and was reassessed. This time, scores qualified him for the learning disabilities resource program. The IEP team was called together to decide Adam's educational needs. Adam was one year behind in reading and one and one-half years behind in written language skills.

As part of this assessment process, assistive technology was discussed. The learning disabilities teacher recommended computer usage in the classroom to address Adam's academic deficits. Adam's parents offered to purchase a home computer for their son to use, while the district would provide one for him at school. It was decided that Adam would use targeted software to practice spelling, and would receive multisensory reading instruction supplemented with CD-ROMs. Language arts homework would be completed with the help of the computer.

The school year proceeded with Adam improving in both reading and writing. He used the computer at school and, after instruction from the learning disabilities teacher, at home. Adam's parents were pleased with his instructional plan.

Scenario 2: The Case of Mayaka

Mayaka, a 16 year-old African-American student, was paralyzed from the waist down as a result of an automobile accident. The injury also caused reduced flexibility in her arms and hands. The IEP team determined Mayaka's special educational needs and developed an IEP. Mayaka received physical therapy for one hour daily during which she would also learn computer skills to assist in her writing activities. The school district committed to supplying two computers, one for school and a matching one for home. Mayaka's parents stated that they were concerned about Mayaka but did not have time to work with her or to assist in the use of the computer at home. The physical therapist recommended a hand device that would hold her palm horizontal and extend her middle finger to make it easier for Mayaka to type with one finger.

The IEP team monitored Mayaka's success in using the hand device to complete her homework. It was noted immediately that Mayaka did not like to use the hand device because it called attention to her disability. She developed a method of typing with the first knuckle of each hand while flopping the fingers away from the keys. Mayaka was generally uncooperative if forced to use the hand device and minimally cooperative if permitted to use her knuckles. Mayaka's mother observed that Mayaka did not use the device at all when her friends played computer games with her at home.

The IEP team met and agreed to discontinue the use of the hand device and allow Mayaka to use her knuckles. The special education consultant stated that Mayaka was generally successful with using the word processor for assignments, but the consultant was concerned that Mayaka was still uncooperative at times when receiving instruction and was not maintaining passing grades. The team revised Mayaka's IEP to reflect more emphasis on supervised completion of homework. In addition, her assignments would be modified to accommodate the time that Mayaka needed to type them.

At the annual review, the IEP team evaluated Mayaka's plan as somewhat successful. While her grades were not outstanding, she passed her courses. Mayaka's parents shared that in addition to being pleased that she had acquired some computer skills, they were happy that she could play games with her friends.

As reflected in these scenarios, successful implementation of home computers may hinge on *real partnerships with families,* in which a range of factors have been considered. In the first scenario, family advocacy played an important role in the child receiving special education services. Also, the importance of computers was well-recognized by the family, contributing to their willingness to purchase one for the child's use at home. In the second scenario, the team failed to determine the family's willingness to teach their child how to use the computer at home. The team also recommended a device for the child to use without considering whether it would draw undue attention to the child's disability. The scenarios make it clear that *supports* are often necessary for families if home computer integration is to be successful. In the first case, a substantial level of family support for implementation of the home computer was present, while less support was provided by the family in the second case.

NEED FOR TRAINING AS A SUPPORT

Family satisfaction with successful implementation of home computers is integrally linked to training as a support service. Assistive technology services have been defined in the *Individuals with Disabilities Education Act of 1997* (IDEA) as "a service that directly assists a child with a disability in the selection, acquisition, or use of an assistive technology device" [§602(2)]. Services include *training* in the use of assistive technology devices (National Information Center for Children and Youth with Disabilities, 1991).

Training in the use of home computers may be especially important when working with families from different cultural backgrounds. For example, African, Hispanic, and Native American children are more likely than Euro- and Asian-American children to have fewer formal learning opportunities at home (Peng, Wright, & Hill, 1995). Because many adults from non-European backgrounds have attended disadvantaged schools, they may reside in stressful environments where there are fewer community and school supports and less reinforcement to succeed in school (Peng et al., 1995). Since many families from non-European cultural backgrounds may expect related service personnel to assume primary responsibility for training related to home computer usage, consideration should be given to what training related service personnel are realistically able to provide to families. This is particularly true given that success in home computer usage may be linked to child and family training before the introduction of the computer in home environments (Kitabachi, 1987).

Several studies during the past decade have indicated that professionals often are not adequately trained at either the pre- or inservice level in the use of assistive technologies (see, e.g., Parette & Van-Biervliet, 1991; Utah Assistive Technology Program, 1991; Illinois Department of Rehabilitation Services, 1990). Other studies have shown that teachers working with students with disabilities fail to use assistive technology devices in classrooms due to lack of training (Derer, Polsgrove, & Rieth, 1996; Izen & Brown, 1991). Swartz (1993) reported on a survey of 234 parents of which 84% of the reporting families had computers in their home environments. Families reported that collaborative planning is necessary to relieve stresses associated with acquiring technology literacy. Others have reported that *lack of training* and resource information, lack of appropriate devices, and lack of resources to maintain equipment are significant barriers to effective use of assistive technology (Parker, Buckley, Truesdell, Riggio, Collins, & Boardman, 1990). Hutinger (1994) found that focus groups of families emphasized financial resources and training as primary challenges in using assistive technology.

Families of children with disabilities are discovering that their knowledge of assistive technology devices is often equivalent to or exceeds that of related services personnel (McNutty, 1988; Parette et al., 1996). This may be frustrating to families who view professionals as experts, particularly for families from non-Euro-American backgrounds who defer their own judgment to that of professionals (Parette & Angelo, 1998).

Professionals taught to use computers find it extremely difficult to keep abreast with the rapid growth of new hardware and software, and effective strategies for their use (Sommerville et al., 1990; Hammel & Angelo, 1996). In addition to increased availability, the newer computer products are often more complex and sophisticated, and may require training strategies for professionals to use them efficiently with families in home settings (Derer et al., 1996; Thorkildsen, 1994).

Many families understand that professionals will have varying levels of training in computers and are willing to work with professionals if honesty regarding levels of proficiency is communicated to the family early in decision-making processes (Parette et al., 1996). Unfortunately, much training for family members regarding the implementation of computers is often provided by professionals who have little or no experience in this area (Behrmann, 1995). When training strategies have proven to be ineffective or when computer integration in the home setting has failed, both children with disabilities and their families may experience frustration and disillusionment (Parette et al., 1996). This can lead to *technology abandonment,* or a decision to not use the computer in the home (Batavia & Hammer, 1989).

CONCLUSION AND IMPLICATIONS

Computers have become integral tools for work in public school and home settings during the last decade. Both educators and families have recognized the tremendous potential of computers to enhance the lives of children with disabilities. With the advent of the new millennium, educators and family members from many cultures will increasingly collaborate as partners on teams to make decisions regarding the provision of computers to children in their respective home environments. New challenges confront teams in the future.

To develop effective partnerships with families, careful consideration must be given to a range of issues. Basic assistive technology decision-making considerations for teams have previously been described in the professional literature (see, e.g., Inge & Shepherd, 1995; Parette et al., 1993). Similarly, specific recommendations for computer decision-making have been reported (Beaver & Mann, 1994; Church, 1992). More recently, family-centered culturally sensitive approaches have been advocated in which child, family, school, technology, and family/cultural concerns become the focus of team decision-making (Hourcade et al., 1997; Judge & Parette, 1998). Generally, it may be concluded that many families across cultures might benefit from the provision of home computers for their children with disabilities, assuming that questions such as those posed in Table 1 have been carefully considered.

It may be that the provision of training as a support to families is the most important factor in the successful implementation of home computers. Families often express frustration with inadequate training and supports provided to them when attempting to use team-prescribed computers in the home setting. Of particular importance may be family-sensitive and user-friendly training provided before introduction of the computer in the home (Kitabachi, 1987).

Families also recognize that related service personnel vary with regard to competency level; however, many feel most professionals need more information relating to availability and use of computers (Parette et al., 1996). Both pre- and inservice programs involved in the training of special education teachers and related service personnel should ensure that professionals are adequately prepared to work collaboratively with families across cultures and to provide the needed supports to families for successful implementation of home computers.

REFERENCES

Ainsa, P. A., Murphy, D., Thouvenelle, S., & Wright, J. L. (1994). Family involvement: Family choices at school and home. In J. L. Wright & D. D. Shade (Eds.), *Young children: Active learners in a technological age* (pp. 121-131). Washington, DC: National Association for the Education of Young Children.

Anderson, P. P., & Fenichel, E. S. (1989). Serving culturally diverse families of infants and toddlers with disabilities. Arlington, VA: National Center for Clinical Infant Programs.

Barcus (Eds.), *Assistive technology: A resource for school, work, and community* (pp. 211-222). Baltimore: Brookes.

Batavia, A. I., & Hammer, G. (1989). Consumer criteria for evaluating assistive devices: Implications for technology transfer. In J. J. Presperin (Ed.), *Proceedings of the 12th Annual Conference of the Rehabilitation Engineering Society of North America* (pp. 194-195). Washington, DC: RESNA Press.

Battle, D. E. (1993). *Communication disorders in multicultural populations.* Boston: Andover Medical Publishers.

Beaver, K. A., & Mann, W. C. (1994). Provider skills for delivering computer access services: An assistive technology team approach. *Technology and Disability, 3,* 109-116.

Behrmann, M. M. (1995). Assistive technology training. In K. Flippo, K. Inge, and J. M. Barcus (Eds.), *Assistive technology: A resource for school, work, and community* (pp. 211-222). Baltimore: Brookes.

Berger, E. H. (1981). *Parents as partners in education. The school and home working together.* St. Louis, MO: Mosby.

Brady, H. (1993). Computers for home learning. *Technology and Learning, 14*(3), 56-59.

Brotherson, M. J., Cook, C. C., & Parette, H. P. (1996). A home-centered approach to assistive technology provision for young children with disabilities. *Focus on Autism and Other Developmental Disabilities, 11*(2), 86-95.

Carver, B. A. (1995). Defining the context of early computer learning for African American males in urban elementary schools. *Journal of Negro Education, 63,* 532-545.

Charp, S. (1996). Home/school connectivity. *T.H.E. Journal, 23*(11), 4.

Church, G. (1992). Adaptive access for microcomputers. In G. Church & S., Glennen (Eds.), *The handbook of assistive technology* (pp. 123-172). San Diego, CA: Singular.

Cole, M., & Griffin, P. (1987). *Contextual factors in education: Improving science and mathematics education for minorities and women.* Madison, WI: Wisconsin Center of Education Research.

Debenham, J., & Smith, G. R. (1994). Computers, schools and families: A radical vision for public education. *T.H.E. Journal, 22*(1), 58-61.

Derer, K., Polsgrove, L., & Rieth, H. (1996). A survey of assistive technology applications in schools and recommendations for practice. *Journal of Special Education Technology, 13,* 62-80.

Dunst, C. J., & Paget, K. D. (1991). Parent-professional partnerships and family empowerment. In M. Fine (Ed.), *Collaborative involvement with parents of exceptional children* (pp. 25-44). Brandon, VT: Clinical Psychology Publishing.

Educational Testing Center. (1985). *Computers, equity and urban schools.* Cambridge, MA: Harvard University.

Fullerton, D. (1995). Partners in learning. *Computing Teacher, 22*(6), 19-20.

Giacquinta, J. B. (1984, June). *Educational microcomputing at home: A comparative case analysis of twenty families with children.* Paper presented at the Conference on Computers in the Home, Washington, DC.

Giacquinta, J. B., & Lane, P. A. (1990). Fifty-one families with computers: A study of children's academic uses of microcomputers at home. *Educational Technology Research and Development, 38*(2), 27-37.

Groce, N. E., & Zola, I. K. (1993). Multiculturalism, chronic illness, and disability. *Pediatrics, 91,* 1048-1055.

Gross, N., Giacquinta, J., & Bernstein, M. (1971). *Implementing organizational innovations.* New York: Basic Books.

Hammel, J. & Angelo, J. (1996). Technology competencies for occupational therapy practitioners. *Assistive Technology, 8,* 34-42.

Harry, B., Allen, N., & McLaughlin, M. (1995). Communication versus compliance: African-American parents' involvement in special education. *Exceptional Children, 61,* 364-377.

Hourcade, J., J., Parette, H. P., & Huer, M. B. (1997). Family and cultural alert! Considerations in assistive technology assessment. *Teaching Exceptional Children, 30*(1), 40-44.

Hourcade, J., J., Parette, H. P., & Huer, M. B. (1997). Family and cultural alert! Considerations in assistive technology assessment. *Teaching Exceptional Children, 30*(1), 40-44.

Hutinger, P. L. (1994). *State of practice: How assistive technologies are used in educational programs of children with multiple disabilities. Final report for the Project Effective Use of Technology to Meet Educational Goals of Children with Disabilities* (No. 180R10020). Macomb, IL: Western Illinois University.

Illinois Department of Rehabilitation Services. (1990). *The strategic plan for the 1990's.* Springfield: Author.

Individuals with Disabilities Education Act Amendments of 1997, P. L. 105-13. (June 4, 1997). 20 U.S.C. § 1400 et seq.

Inge, K. J., & Shepherd, J. (1995). Assistive technology applications and strategies for school system personnel. In K. F. Flippo, K. J. Inge, & J. M. Barcus (Eds.), *Assistive technology. A resource for school, work, and community* (pp. 133-166). Baltimore: Brookes.

Judge, S. L., & Parette, H. P. (1998). Assistive technology decision-making strategies. In S. L. Judge, & H. P. Parette (Eds.), *Assistive technology for young children with disabilities: A guide to providing family-centered services* (pp. 127-147). Cambridge, MA: Brookline.

Kitabachi, G. (1987, November). *Evaluation of the Apple classroom of tomorrow.* Paper presented at the Sixteenth Annual Meeting of the Mid-South Educational Research Association, Mobile, AL (ERIC Document Reproduction Service No. ED 295 600).

Klimes-Dougan, B., Lopez, J. A., Nelson, P., & Adelman, H. S. (1992). Two studies of low-income parents' involvement in schooling. *The Urban Review, 24*(3), 185-202.

Lee, A. (1997). Lifelong learning: Workforce development and economic success. (ERIC Document Reproduction Service No. ED 411 895).

Lockard, J., Abrams, P. D., & Many, W. A. (1997). *Microcomputers for twenty-first century educators* (4th ed.). New York: Longman.

Male, M. (1994). *Technology for inclusion. Meeting the special needs of all students.* (2nd ed.). Boston: Allyn and Bacon.

McNutty, B. (1988, May). *Assistive technology: The Colorado effort* (Senate Report

100-438). Paper and testimony presented to the Senate Subcommittee on the Handicapped, Senator Thomas Harkin (Chairperson), Washington, D.C.

Milone, M. N., & Salpeter, J. (1996). Technology and equity issues. *Technology and Learning, 16*(4), 38-47.

National Information Center for Children and Youth with Disabilities. (1991). Related services for school-age children with disabilities. *NICHCY News Digest, 1*, 1-24.

Office of Technology Policy. (1997). *America's new deficit: The shortage of information technology workers.* (ERIC Document Reproduction Service No. ED 412360).

Ogbu, J. (1987). Cultural influences on plasticity in human development. In J. J. Gallagher & C. T. Ramey (Eds.), *The malleability of children* (pp. 155-169). Baltimore: Brookes.

Parette, H. P. (1997). Assistive technology devices and services. *Education and Training in Mental Retardation and Developmental Disabilities, 32*, 267-280.

Parette, H. P., & Angelo, D. H. (1998). Impact of assistive technology devices on families. In S. L. Judge, & H. P. Parette (Eds.), *Assistive technology for young children with disabilities: A guide to providing family-centered services* (pp. 184-210). Cambridge, MA: Brookline.

Parette, H. P., & Brotherson, M. J. (1996). Family participation in assistive technology assessment for young children with disabilities. *Education and Training in Mental Retardation and Developmental Disabilities, 31*(1), 29-43.

Parette, H. P., Brotherson, M. J., Hoge, D. R., & Hostetler, S. A. (1996, December). *Family-centered augmentative and alternative communication issues: Implications across cultures.* Paper presented to the International Early Childhood Conference on Children with Special Needs, Phoenix, AZ.

Parette, H. P., Hourcade, J. J., & VanBiervliet, A. (1993). Selection of appropriate technology for children with disabilities. *Teaching Exceptional Children, 25*(3), 18-22.

Parette, H. P., & VanBiervliet, A. (1991). Rehabilitation technology issues for infants and young children with disabilities: A preliminary examination. *Journal of Rehabilitation, 57*, 27-36.

Parker, S., Buckley, W., Truesdell, M., Riggio, M., Collins, M., & Boardman, B. (1990). Barriers to the use of assistive technology with children: A survey. *Journal of Visual Impairment & Blindness, 84*, 532-533.

Peng, S. S., Wright, D., & Hill, S. T. (1995). *Understanding racial-ethnic differences in secondary school science and mathematics achievement.* Washington, DC: National Center for Education Statistics.

Piller, C. (1992). Separate realities. *MacWorld, September,* 218-230.

RESNA Technical Assistance Project. (1992). *Assistive technology and the individualized education program.* Washington, DC: RESNA Press.

Resta, P. (1992). Organizing education for minorities: Enhancing minority access and use of the new information technologies in higher education. *Education and Computing, 8*, 119-127.

Rogers, E. (1983). *Diffusion of innovations* (3rd ed.). New York: Basic Books.

Rosado, L. R. (1994). Promoting partnerships with minority parents: A revolution in today's school restructuring efforts. *The Journal of Educational Issues of Language Minority Students, 14*, 241-254.

Ross, S. M., Smith, L. J., Morrison, G. R., O'Dell, J., Perry, G., Martin, J., & Lohr, L. (1989). *What happens after ACOT: Outcomes for program graduates one-year later.* (ERIC Document Reproduction Service No. ED 316 196).

Scherer, M. J. (1996). *Living in the state of stuck. How technology impacts the lives of people with disabilities* (2nd ed.). Cambridge, MA: Brookline.

Shashaani, L. (1994). Socioeconomic status, parents' sex-role stereotypes, and the gender gap in computing. *Journal of Research on Computing in Education, 26,* 433-451.

Simpson, R. L. (1996). *Working with parents and families of exceptional children and youth. Techniques for successful conferencing and collaboration* (3rd ed.). Austin, TX: PRO-ED.

Somerville, N. J., Wilson, D. J., Shanfield, K. J., Mack, W. (1990). A survey of the assistive technology training needs of occupational therapists. *Assistive Technology, 2,* 41-49.

Soto, G., Huer, M. B., & Taylor, O. (1997). Multicultural issues. In L. L. Lloyd, D. H. Fuller, & H. H. Arvidson (Eds.), *Augmentative and alternative communication* (pp. 406-413). Boston: Allyn and Bacon.

Stainback, W., & Stainback, S. (1990). *Support networks for inclusive schooling.* Baltimore: Brookes.

Swartz, A. (1993). *Computer or related technology use at home by children and youth with disabilities: A survey of parents.* Unpublished doctoral dissertation, Teachers College, Columbia University.

The Americans with Disabilities Act of 1990, P. L. 101-336. (July 26, 1990). 42 U. S. C. A. §§122101 et seq.

Thorkildsen, R. (1994). *Research synthesis on quality and availability of assistive technology devices. Technical Report No. 7.* Eugene, OR: Oregon University, College of Education, National Center to Improve the Tools of Educators.

Times Mirror Center for the People and the Press. (1994). *Technology in the American household.* Washington, DC: Author.

Tornatsky, L. (1983). *The process of technological change.* Washington, DC: National Science Foundation.

Trachtman, L. E., Spirek, M. M., Sparks, G. G., & Stohl, C. (1991, October/November). *Response to a community-based information and communication system.* Paper presented at the Annual Meeting of the Speech Communication Association, Atlanta, GA.

Turnbull, R., & Turnbull, A. (1978). *Parents speak out: The view from the other side of the mirror.* Columbus, OH: Merrill.

Ullery, L. V. (1993). *Developing and sustaining early literacy experiences for prekindergarten children through a systematic program of home/school involvement.* (ERIC Document Reproduction Service No. ED 362 852).

Utah Assistive Technology Program. (1991). *Utah assistive technology providers survey: Individuals, groups, agencies.* Logan, UT: Utah State University, Center for Disabilities.

Wehman, P. (Ed.). (1993). *The ADA mandate for social change.* Baltimore: Brookes.

Wilhelm, A. G. (1997). *Buying into the computer age: A look at the Hispanic middle class.* (ERIC Document Reproduction Service No. ED 414 360).

Computer Support for School-Based Team Consultation

Seth Aldrich

Syracuse City Schools

SUMMARY. School-based consultation teams have been implemented in a variety of ways to address students' academic and behavioral difficulties while supporting teachers. Recent research has provided information that may benefit the school-based team consultation process. Computer software offers an effective and efficient means of guiding diverse team members through a comprehensive consultation process, generating intervention scripts, tailoring data collection to student needs, as well as recording and communicating information shared during team consultation. *[Article copies available for a fee from The Haworth Document Delivery Service: 1-800-342-9678. E-mail address: <getinfo@haworthpressinc.com> Website: <http://www.HaworthPress.com>]*

KEYWORDS. Teams, consultation, computers

INTRODUCTION

There are a wide variety of school-based consultation teams that make decisions for individual students who are experiencing difficulties. The composition of these teams, their meeting agendas, as well as their procedures for problem solving reflect belief systems concerning student adjustment in school and have a strong influence on the way

---

Address correspondence to: Dr. Seth Aldrich, 209 Carlton Road, Syracuse, NY. 13207.

[Haworth co-indexing entry note]: "Computer Support for School-Based Team Consultation." Aldrich, Seth. Co-published simultaneously in *Special Services in the Schools* (The Haworth Press, Inc.) Vol. 17, No. 1/2, 2001, pp. 115-129; and: *Computers in the Delivery of Special Education and Related Services: Developing Collaborative and Individualized Learning Environments* (ed: Louis J. Kruger) The Haworth Press, Inc., 2001, pp. 115-129. Single or multiple copies of this article are available for a fee from The Haworth Document Delivery Service [1-800-342-9678, 9:00 a.m. - 5:00 p.m. (EST). E-mail address: getinfo@haworth pressinc.com].

problems are solved. For example, a team comprised of school support staff such as psychologists, social workers and speech/language pathologists who consult to diagnose student difficulties within an evaluation of special education eligibility, approach the problem solving process very differently than teams comprised of teachers and support staff who collaborate with the student's teacher to provide strategies, resources and support for student adjustment in the regular or special education setting. While the agenda of the first type of team is typically to identify a student deficit and make a special education determination, the second type of team focuses more on what can happen within regular education to help the student academically, behaviorally and or emotionally. Recent school-based consultation literature (Witt & Martens, 1988; McKee & Witt, 1990; Rosenfield, 1992; Elliot & Sheridan, 1992) has focused on consultation strategies that support student adjustment through modifying aspects of the instructional environment that are likely to impact positively on the defined concern. Computer software may be incorporated into the team consultation process to (a) facilitate a comprehensive team meeting, (b) provide examples of wording to facilitate a problem solving process, (c) provide intervention scripts, (d) tailor data collection devices, and (e) record information shared at meetings for effective communication. Software mediation of the consultative process which adheres to what is known as being 'best practice' procedures, as well as resources provided by the software may support the implementation of interventions that lead to observable student outcomes.

This article will discuss recent literature relevant to school-based consultation teams that describe recommended practices, as well as challenges to successful team functioning. In doing so, a school-based consultation team model will be described that incorporates research-based components to a team consultation process. The use of team consultation software to assist school-based consultation teams in Syracuse, New York will be described. Finally, cautions and ethical considerations when using software to support school-based consultation teams will be discussed.

CURRENT INTEREST IN SCHOOL-BASED CONSULTATION TEAMS

There has been a recent surge of interest in teams that provide resources, support and intervention strategies to teachers of students who are experiencing difficulties in the classroom. Much of this interest stems from concerns over the rapidly rising special education referral rates, disappointment with the effectiveness of special education services (Kavale, 1990), and the limited utility of the psychoeducational evaluation process to provide information that ultimately benefits students (Gresham, MacMillan & Bocian, 1998). Benefits of consultation teams that include teachers as members (as opposed to traditional consultation between a single 'specialist' and a classroom teacher) include: increased referent power that teacher members may have (Tingstrom, Little & Stewart, 1990), and increased number of colleagues who can provide support within the school community (Rosenfield & Gravois, 1996). Furthermore, teachers understand the daily challenges that other teachers face and may be in a better position than an "expert" (i.e., school psychologist) to suggest ideas to colleagues. While the names, procedures and preparation of school-based consultation teams are different, most espouse the basic elements of school-based consultation teams which follows the behavioral consultation model defined by Bergan (1977): (a) problem identification, (b) problem analysis, (c) goal setting, (d) intervention planning, and (e) outcome evaluation.

POTENTIAL OBSTACLES TO IMPLEMENTING SCHOOL-BASED CONSULTATION TEAMS: OPPORTUNITIES FOR IMPROVEMENT

Whereas the practice of consultation in schools is quite popular among school psychologists, teachers and administrators, some authors have been critical of the assumptions about its efficacy (Witt & Martens, 1988; Gresham, 1989; Noell & Witt, 1996; Witt, 1997). Questions concerning commonly held assumptions about consultation include: (a) the notion that indirect service delivery is superior to direct intervention, (b) a collaborative approach to consultation is superior to a more directive or 'expert' model, (c) verbal interactions are sufficient to change instructional practices, and (d) the imposition of individually tailored interventions to modify student behavior as opposed to modifying existing instructional practices. These challenges to commonly held assumptions about consultation point out the work that is needed to develop and understand a process of effective school-based intervention teams. Software programs that mediate consultation should incorporate procedures known to be effective, provide strategies to assist teams with obstacles, and carefully consider consultation issues that are yet unresolved. The section below addresses challenges to assumptions about consultation and describe obstacles to effective team consultation.

Collaborative versus Expert Approaches to Consultation

The assumption that a collaborative approach is superior to an expert approach to consultation, as well as what constitutes a collaborative approach, has been recently debated (Kratochwill, Bergan, Sheridan & Elliot, 1998; Noell, Gresham & Duhon, 1998). Although it makes sense that a consultation process maintain a high level of respect and support, it is not known that a more directive or 'expert system' (i.e., an expert software program advising interventions based on the prioritized problem endorsed) would be ill advised in consultative situations. Consideration of choice, flexibility and collaboration would be important when designing software that mediates the consultation process.

Meeting Agendas That Promote Problem Solving

One obstacle to improving the school-based consultation teams' process is a mind set that student difficulties stem from fixed characteristics or deficits. Fundamental attribution bias as described in social psychology (Harvey, Arkin, Gleason & Johnston, 1974) suggests that people typically attribute difficulties experienced by others as the result of that person's own deficiencies while attributing their own difficulties to situational factors. Fundamental attribution bias supports the notion that academic difficulties experienced by students are too often attributed to student deficits rather than situational factors. Research suggests that different ways of describing student difficulties can influence problem attributions about students and treatment selections to address student difficulties (Tombari & Bergan, 1978; Gutkin, 1986; McKee & Witt, 1990; Aldrich & Martens, 1993). Wording used during team consultation can also influence teachers' acceptability of the process. It is important that software mediating consultation use common sense language and limited jargon (Witt, Moe, Gutkin & Andrews, 1984).

Time to Train School-Based Consultation Teams

Consultation skills, as well as the way in which consultation is conducted, vary widely (Kratochwill & Van Someren, 1985). A considerable amount of training and support is required for school-based consultation teams to engage in a comprehensive problem-solving process. Team members need to know topics such as: how to operationalize and prioritize student difficulties, goal setting, implementation of interventions that work, and formative evaluation. For example, Instructional Consultation Teams (Rosenfield & Gravois, 1996) are comprised of a variety of teachers and support staff who are trained to provide comprehensive school-based consultation. The approach is appealing because it provides a training for teachers and support staff alike to learn a comprehensive school-based problem-solving process, including evaluation of intervention outcomes. Unfortunately, the Instructional Consultation Team model requires one full week of training for team members at the outset, as well as ongoing training activities throughout the year. Many school districts would find this investment prohibitive to implement and maintain.

Prepared Intervention "Packages" for Commonly Occurring Student Difficulties

Given the time and resources that it requires to train school-based consultation teams, as well as the time that it requires to operate teams during the school day, it is tempting (and perhaps appropriate at times) to 'give' consultees prepared intervention packages to address commonly occurring student difficulties. While there are potential benefits to a small fixed menu of effective interventions for consultees to implement, packaged approaches have been found to be inflexible (Rosenfield, 1992). It is important that resources provide adequate choice for consultees. Tingstrom, Little and Stewart (1990) suggest that when consultees are stripped of choice during consultation they may experience reactance and resist the consultative process.

Intervention Follow Through

Perhaps one of the greatest challenges to the consultation process has to do with treatment integrity (Gresham, 1989; Witt, 1997). Abundant research suggests that most teachers do not follow through with interventions decided upon during consultation (Wickstrom, Jones, LaFluer & Witt, 1998; Witt, 1997). Thus, school-based consultation team procedures that promote interventions that can and will be followed through, provide support to teachers, and monitor treatment integrity (investigating whether the intervention was implemented as planned) are essential to positive student outcomes.

Fallibility of Intervention Strategies

Even when interventions are conducted faithfully there is no guarantee that they will be effective for a given student. A meta-analysis by Kavale (1990) provides evidence that interventions vary in their effectiveness for individual students and that many interventions thought to be very effective are generally not. The main point of the Kavale study is that no one can assume that any intervention will be effective for an individual student. Formative evaluation of outcomes coupled with appropriate modifications can increase the probability that interventions will produce the desired student changes. Although this step is crucial in the consultation process, it is frequently overlooked or neglected when resources are scarce.

EMPIRICALLY SUPPORTED COMPONENTS OF CONSULTATION

Several strategies can be implemented within a consultation process to increase opportunities for positive consultee and or student outcomes. These strategies involve techniques of identifying and understanding academic and or behavioral difficulties in ways that (a) improve intervention choices, (b) support teacher follow through with interventions, and (c) formatively evaluate the success of interventions. It is important to recognize these strategies when developing and training school-based consultation teams.

Problem Identification

Clearly identifying student difficulties in measurable terms is an essential aspect of the consultation process from a behavioral perspective (Bergan & Tombari, 1975, 1976). Concerns that are clearly identified in observable terms help teams to prioritize, set goals, identify interventions that will directly address student difficulties, and often help teams to identify methods of evaluating outcomes.

Understanding Issues Underlying Student Difficulties

Understanding factors that are functionally related to academic and behavioral problems increases the chances that interventions selected will be effective (Daly, Lentz & Boyer, 1996). It is more beneficial to identify contributing factors, through techniques such as functional assessment, that can be controlled in school (e.g., the impact of instructional match on academic difficulties, or setting events that trigger behavioral difficulties) than to assess more 'fixed' traits that do not contribute to solutions (e.g., IQ test results). Understanding the functions of problem behaviors is a substantial new requirement in the reauthorization of IDEA that will likely require training and support for practitioners to conduct in a useful manner.

Increasing Intervention Follow Through

Intervention scripts that have been collaboratively (Ehrhardt, Barnett, Lentz, Stollar, & Reifin, 1996) developed by researchers or practitioners (Hiralall & Martens, 1998) can increase teacher follow through with interventions. Providing teachers with feedback about their intervention attempts also enhances treatment integrity (Jones, Wickstrom & Friman 1997; Martens, Hiralall & Bradley, 1997). These findings suggest that scripts detailing specific steps of intervention strategies proposed at school-based consultation team meetings would be very useful to achieving desired outcomes.

Monitoring Student Progress in Response to Intervention Strategies

Techniques for monitoring student progress have been found to be associated with increased student progress in the area monitored (Fuchs & Fuchs, 1986). Monitoring is important for teachers as well as teams to know when treatments have produced the desired results (Kavale, 1990). Although several formative evaluation tools (e.g., curriculum-based assessment and teacher behavior report cards) have been developed to monitor intervention effectiveness, consultation team members may not be familiar with them.

RATIONALE FOR TEAM CONSULTATION SOFTWARE

Software that assists teams through the consultation process while recording meeting information could incorporate effective strategies and address limitations described in the above literature review.

Steps of a problem solving process (problem identification including data-based decision making, problem analysis, plan generation and intervention monitoring) (Bergan, 1977), could be scripted so that a variety of professionals can actively participate in team consultation. In addition, the appropriate software can help staff (e.g., teachers) with high referent power, but relatively little experience and training in consultation, to follow a consultation process in a thorough manner. It should be noted that computer software cannot create an atmosphere of collegiality, respect and active listening that is essential to school-based consultation teams. Nonetheless, software could guide users to avoid use of jargon and provide teacher friendly language, while at the same time facilitate planning of specific interventions relevant to data collection throughout the problem solving process.

Team consultation software could collect all relevant information generated at a problem solving meeting. The software would provide prompts for the type of information that should be shared at the meeting, and keep the meeting focused on a positive solution for the student. While several authors have discussed the importance of a collaborative free exchange of ideas (Conoley & Conoley, 1982; Rosenfield, 1992), little empirical information has been gathered about aspects of the consultation process that lead to optimal student outcomes. It has been suggested that in the spirit of collaboration and trust, data driven decision making and accountability has been sacrificed (Witt, 1997). Teachers need to feel supported in the process and provided with positive feedback. However, a process that reinforces teachers to continue ineffective teaching practices is inimical to producing positive changes for students.

A scripted consultation process, mediated either through forms or software, has several advantages. The team is guided through various steps of the process that may be unfamiliar or uncomfortable, yet essential to the success of the case. For example, it may be uncomfortable for teachers engaged in consultation with a colleague to check whether the intervention is being implemented as prescribed. A structured, non-negotiable process assures that these 'uncomfortable' steps are covered, yet absolves consulting teachers of a role that may be perceived as distrustful. Furthermore, because the step is built in as a way of supporting the teacher in his or her intervention efforts after the meeting, the negative connotation of 'integrity checking' is alleviated.

Users who select research based interventions from an intervention menu could be provided with scripts that specify important steps to collaboratively developed strategies. These prewritten scripts could assure that all necessary treatment components are included so that chances for intervention success are increased. Likewise, treatment integrity checklists could accompany interventions already provided by the software, or be created at the meeting for customized interventions.

Evaluation of intervention outcomes is an essential step in the consultation process. Although several assessment strategies have been developed (i.e., curriculum-based assessment and direct systematic behavioral observation) that allow teams to monitor student progress subsequent to interventions, high quality outcome measures are frequently omitted by school-based teams. Team consultation software could increase use of quality formative evaluation techniques in two ways. First, a software program could prompt goals in such a way that the method to assess would be quite clear (e.g., "Johnny will read 35 correctly read words in the 2-1 basal reader with 85% accuracy by April 10"). Secondly, team consultation software could prompt the necessary selection and planning of techniques for assessing student outcomes at the appropriate stage of the meeting.

Team consultation software also could provide an efficient means of collecting and sharing information. A summary of the student background information, defined problem, baseline data, intervention plan and intervention monitoring plan can be printed and distributed immediately after the meeting. Otherwise, it may take several days for referring teachers and team members to receive meeting summaries, intervention scripts and treatment integrity checklists.

Given the lack of consistency in how school-based consultation is currently practiced (Kratochwill & Van Someren, 1985), software may also prove useful in developing a more consistent process for some types of research about consultation.

TEAM CONSULTATION SOFTWARE (WRIGHT & ALDRICH, 1997)

Currently, there are nine elementary schools in the Syracuse city school district which are involved with the School-Based Intervention Team (SBIT) project. SBIT teams in Syracuse are comprised of approximately eight school staff, many of whom are classroom teachers. The SBIT process borrows heavily from the behavioral/instructional consultation model, and the SBIT planning team has worked to incorporate best practice consultation components with limited human resource or staff development funds. SBIT meetings are highly structured with meeting notes forms to assure that all steps in the problem solving process are covered during the meeting. The SBIT team facilitator, recorder, timekeeper, and case liaison roles rotate so that all team members have a chance to develop necessary skills and share responsibilities.

A prototype Team Consultation Software program (Wright & Aldrich, 1997) created using HyperCard ™ software, has been used in SBIT meetings. Team Consultation Software collects student background information and leads the user through a series of screens that encompasses the problem solving process as defined by the Syracuse City Schools SBIT project. Consultees have the choice to enter information through either selecting from an extensive menu of preentered information (e.g., different types of student difficulties worded in clear measurable terms and intervention choices complete with step by step procedures), or by typing information into text fields. The software also contains scripts of intervention procedures and intervention evaluation practices that can help consultation teams to incorporate effective components of consultation. After teams complete the process using the software, a narrative report that includes all of the information input during the meeting is generated and printed. Options for printing executive summaries, complete reports, and intervention scripts are available.

The Team Consultation Software was developed for several reasons. Teams had reported that the process for documenting all of the information required by the SBIT process was cumbersome. It was believed that the software would enable teams to input information efficiently (i.e., through selecting preentered responses) making information recording easier. The software also provided guidance and model responses for (a) problem descriptions, (b) antecedent, concurrent and consequent events associated with problems, (c) goal statements, (d) intervention scripts, (e) procedures to measure intervention effectiveness, and (f) treatment integrity checklists.

After the software was developed, teams were taught how to use the software. In addition, members of the SBIT planning team assisted teams through their initial attempts to use the software. Information about the utility of the software was collected in three different ways. First, the developers worked directly with teams while using the software, asking SBIT members to provide feedback about the software. An end of year SBIT evaluation questionnaire also asked for feedback about the software. Finally, a 'bug' program built into the software enabled users to write down feedback about any difficulties encountered while they used the software. Modifications based on consumer feedback included: rephrasing questions for increased clarity, increasing navigation flexibility, and a clipboard to record relevant information not prompted by the software.

Teams reported that advantages to using the software included helping them to follow the SBIT process in its entirety and having thorough documentation of the information collected at the meeting. Disadvantages included difficulties associated with the lock-step meeting process that the software demanded (information had to be input according to the sequence of the program), and the fact that the software sometimes interfered with a free flow of ideas within a particular stage of consultation and dominated the consultation meeting.

As discussed earlier in this article, team consultation needs to be flexible within a structure that assures appropriate information collection and intervention planning. Team consultation software helps teams to follow the recommended sequence of consultation (c.g., prompting teams to identify and prioritize problems before deciding on interventions) while allowing flexibility in terms of information shared and decisions made within the various consultation stages. Although a strength of the Team Consultation Software prototype version is that teams need to progress through the entire consultation process, a weakness is that there is little flexibility within the consultation stages. Furthermore, it is only available to teams with a Macintosh computer. The Team Consultation Software prototype version can be downloaded from the SBIT web site: < www.scsd.k12.ny.us/sbit/index.htm >.

FUTURE DIRECTIONS

A future version of Team Consultation Software could link specifically identified problems with corresponding reasons for their occurrence (or factors that support, or are functionally related to the problem). Team consultation software would be able to suggest antecedent or consequent events that have been shown to support various behavioral difficulties. Although reasons for student difficulties may be multifaceted, school-based consultation teams need to focus on factors that are related to improving a student's functioning in school.

The software could have several features intended to further enhance the consultation process. The software could provide 'smart links' that connect specifically identified problems (selected from a menu of commonly occurring problems) with intervention choices likely to address those problems. Thus, problems and their functions identified during earlier stages of the meeting can be electronically linked to corresponding interventions.

For example, if low student engagement due to the student escaping difficult work was identified and prioritized as the most important problem, interventions likely to produce the desired changes (e.g., providing a more appropriate instructional match) could be made available to the user. Interventions chosen by the team could have scripts that assure that resources (i.e., time, training and materials) and essential treatment components are described at the meeting. Checklists detailing intervention steps can also be available so that treatment integrity can be evaluated.

Although ongoing assessment of student response to interventions is a crucial aspect of instructional consultation, the development of assessment measures can be very time intensive and impractical for teams. Team consultation software could contain applications that enable teams to tailor formative evaluation techniques such as teacher behavior report cards and curriculum based assessment (CBA) reading readiness and math probes to specific student needs. Such an application could include directions and formats for conducting assessments that increase utility as well as accuracy of the assessment. Currently, a behavior report card generator and curriculum based assessment probe generator are available on the SBIT website.

ETHICAL CONSIDERATIONS

It is important that school staff who use team consultation software without training understand its limitations. Staff who use software in 'high stakes' decision making processes (i.e., a process that might lead to a special education designation based on failure to respond to several implemented and evaluated treatments) need to have training in consultation beyond the assistance that the software provides. The availability of team consultation software could give school staff a false sense of expertise in consultation. Furthermore, process aspects of the team consultation (i.e., developing a collegial, supportive atmosphere) that are believed to be essential to positive consultation outcomes could be neglected if 'information input' dominated the meeting.

School staff engaged in any form of individual or team consultation need to be aware of fundamental ethical issues involved. Because software would enable school staff who lack formal training in consultation to engage in a problem solving process with other staff, some professional and ethical guidelines associated with formal consultation (e.g., confidentiality) could be compromised. It would be important for schools using team consultation software to have some training in consultation before using it.

Information obtained during school-based consultation is confidential. Software containing consultee and student information, as well as paper copies should be kept in a secure location.

Information about research supporting various aspects of the software, as well as limitations to the process, should be provided to the user. For example, users need to know that even though software may prompt suggested interventions that are linked with problem identification and problem analysis information, the best human or electronic consultant can not assure that the suggested interventions will be the best way to handle the problem.

In summary, computer software has potential to facilitate a comprehensive consultation process integrating effective, research based consultation strategies. Furthermore, software can help teams to link interventions to prioritized student difficulties, provide resources for intervention implementation, and assist with clear communication of meeting results.

REFERENCES

Aldrich, S. F. & Martens, B. K. (1993). The effects of behavioral analysis versus instructional environment information on teachers' perceptions. *School Psychology Quarterly, 8,* 110-124.

Bergan, J. (1977). *Behavioral consultation.* Columbus, OH: Merrill.

Bergan, J. & Tombari, M. (1975). The analysis of verbal interactions occurring during consultation. *Journal of School Psychology, 13,* 209-226.

Bergan, J. & Tombari, M. (1976). Consultant skill and efficiency and the implementation and outcome of consultation. *Journal of School Psychology, 14,* 3-14.

Conoley, J. C., & Conoley, C. W. (1982). *School consultation: A guide to practice and training.* Elmsford, NY: Pergamon.

Daly, E. J., Lentz, F. E., & Boyer, J. (1996). The instructional hierarchy: A conceptual model for understanding the effective components of reading interventions. *School Psychology Quarterly, 11,* 369-386.

Ehrhardt, K. E., Barnett, D. W., Lentz F. E., Stollar, S. A., & Reifin, L. H. (1996).

Innovative methodology in ecological consultation: Use of scripts to promote treatment acceptability and integrity. *School Psychology Quarterly, 2* 149-168.

Elliot, S. N. & Sheridan, S. M. (1992). Consultation and teaming: Problem solving among educators, parents, and support personnel. *The Elementary School Journal, 92,* 315-338.

Fuchs, L. & Fuchs, D. (1986). Effects of systematic formative evaluation in student achievement: A meta-analysis. *Exceptional Children, 51,* 199-208.

Gresham, F. M. (1989). Assessment of treatment integrity in school consultation and pre-referral intervention. *School Psychology Review, 18,* 37-50.

Gresham, F. M., MacMillan, D. L., & Bocian, K. M. (1998). Agreement between school study team decisions and authoritative definitions in classification of students at risk for mild disabilities. *School Psychology Quarterly, 13,* 181-191.

Gutkin, T. B. (1986). Consultees' perceptions of variables relating to the outcomes of school-based consultation interactions. *Schools Psychology Review, 16,* 306-316.

Harvey, J. H., Arkin, R. M., Gleason, J. M., & Johnston, S. (1974). Effect of expected and observed outcome of an action on the differential casual attributions of actor and observer. *Journal of Personality, 42,* 62-77.

Hiralall, A. S. & Martens, B. K. (1998). Teaching classroom management skills to preschool staff: The effects of scripted consultation sequences on teacher and student behavior. *School Psychology Quarterly, 13,* 94-115.

Jones, K. M., Wickstrom, K. F., & Friman, P. C. (1997). The effects of observational feedback on treatment integrity in school based behavioral consultation. *School Psychology Quarterly, 12,* 316-326.

Kavale, K. (1990). The effectiveness of special education. In T. B. Gutkin & C. R. Reynolds (Eds.), *The handbook of school psychology* (2nd ed.) (pp. 868-898). New York: Wiley.

Kratochwill, T. R., & Van Someren, K. R. (1985). Barriers to treatment success in behavioral consultation: Current limitations and future directions. *Journal of School Psychology, 23,* 225-239.

Kratochwill, T. R., Bergan, J. R., Sheridan, S. M., & Elliot, S. N. (1998). Assumptions of behavioral consultation: After all is said and done more has been done than said. *School Psychology Quarterly, 13,* 63-80.

Martens, B. K., Hiralall, A. S., & Bradley, T. A. (1997). Improving student behavior through goal setting and feedback. *School Psychology Quarterly, 12,* 33-41.

McKee, W. T, & Witt, J. C. (1990). Effective teaching:A review of instructional and environmental variables. In T. B. Gutkin & C. R. Reynolds (Eds.), *The handbook of school psychology* (2nd ed.) (pp. 823-894). New York: Wiley.

Noell, G. H. & Witt, J. C. (1996). A critical reevaluation of five fundamental assumptions underlying behavioral consultation. *School Psychology Quarterly, 11,* 189-203.

Noell, G. H., Gresham, F. M., & Duhon, G. (1998). Fundamental agreements and epistemological differences in differentiating what was said from what was done in behavioral consultation. *School Psychology Quarterly, 13,* 81-88.

Rosenfield, S. (1992). Developing school-based consultation teams: A design for organizational change *School Psychology Quarterly 7,* 27-46.

Rosenfield, S. A., & Gravois, T. A. (1996). *Instructional consultation teams: Collaboration for change.* New York: Guilford Press.

Tingstrom, D. H., Little, S. G., & Stewart, K. J. (1990). School Consultation from social psychological perspective: A review. *Psychology in the Schools, 27,* 41-50.

Tombari & Bergan (1978). Consultant cues and teacher verbalizations, judgments and expectancies concerning children's adjustment problems. *Journal of School Psychology, 16,* 212-219.

Wickstrom, K. F., Jones, K. M., LaFluer, L. H., & Witt, J. C. (1998). An analysis of treatment integrity in school based behavioral consultation. *School Psychology Quarterly, 13,* 141-154.

Witt, J. C. (1997). Talk is not cheap. *School Psychology Quarterly, 12,* 281-292.

Witt, J. C. & Martens, B. K. (1988). Problems with problem solving consultation: A reanalysis of assumptions, methods and goals. *School Psychology Review, 17,* 211-226.

Witt, J. C., Moe, G., Gutkin, T., & Andrews, L. (1984). The effect of saying the same thing in different ways: The problem of language and jargon in school-based consultation. *Journal of School Psychology, 22,* 361-367.

Wright, J. A. & Aldrich, S. F. (1997). Team Consultation Software.

Index